Fearne Cotton
The Biography

NIGEL GOODALL

Fearne Cotton

The Biography

The Amazing Story of Britain's Brightest Young TV Star

JOHN BLAKE

Published by John Blake Publishing Ltd,
3 Bramber Court, 2 Bramber Road,
London W14 9PB, England

www.blake.co.uk

First published in hardback in 2008

ISBN: 978 1 84454 584 1

British Library Cataloguing-in-Publication Data:

A catalogue record for this book is available from the British Library.

Design by www.envydesign.co.uk

Printed in the UK by CPI William Clowes Beccles NR34 7TL

1 3 5 7 9 10 8 6 4 2

Papers used by John Blake Publishing are natural, recyclable products made
from wood grown in sustainable forests. The manufacturing processes conform to
the environmental regulations of the country of origin.

Every attempt has been made to contact the relevant copyright-holders, but some
were unobtainable. We would be grateful if the appropriate people could contact us.

PRAISE FOR NIGEL GOODALL'S PREVIOUS BOOKS

Kylie Naked (with Jenny Stanley-Clarke)

'To their credit, the authors don't try and shatter her girl-next-door image and her career is covered in almost bang-up-to-date detail, including an extra chapter to take account of her recent success with *Can't Get You Out Of My Head* and her fantastic performance at the 2002 Brit Awards. Hopefully the Princess of Pop will find time one day to pen her autobiography, but until then *Kylie Naked* is as thorough and an enjoyable account of her life as you could possibly want.'

Jonathan Weir, Amazon.co.uk

Winona Ryder – The Biography

'Overall, this biography is a very interesting read. The chronological nature of the book is especially useful if referring back to it at a later point, and there is also a filmography and a list of Winona's awards and nominations at the back. Combined with this is a comprehensive index making it easy to find references to particular films and people, should you wish to do so. Although it can never be as insightful as an authorised biography, or indeed an autobiography, this book is just as good as it can be. By collating information from a diverse selection of sources, Nigel Goodall has produced a good book that is well worth reading whether you're a fan of Winona Ryder or not.'

T. J. Mackey, Dooyou Online

What's Eating Johnny Depp

'Nigel Goodall does it again! He was the author of an estimable book about Kylie Minogue, one of the only books about the Australian pop princess to try to dig behind the myth and to get the facts right. Try to get it if you possibly can, it's called *Kylie Naked*. With his life of Johnny Depp we can see Goodall once again hovering over the glamour stars of US cinema (he has written previously on one of Depp's leading ladies, the also diminutive trouble magnet Winona Ryder) and coming up with an intriguing portrait of a very talented man whose only trouble is corralling in all his passions. He was a teen star in *Jump Street* and a horror franchise, and then the director John Waters took a chance on him and cast him in his hillbilly epic *Cry Baby*. Depp had enough smarts to say hell yes to this offer and before the movie had ended audiences fell in love with his goofy charm and of course, the shot where his pants fall off and he's left to wander in his jockey shorts. Depp showed great depth in a variety of independent and studio movies, including *Donnie Brasco*, but it wasn't until recently that he was thought of in terms of being able to 'open' a movie. Throughout this chequered career (which includes a directorial debut of his own, apparently dire enough to doom a lesser man) Goodall keeps up as best as he can, and both of them end up on the same page. I'm looking forward to a remake of *A Star Is Born* with Depp and Minogue, it would be utterly of the present moment ...'

Kevin Killan, Amazon.com

To the next generation of telly addicts…

…my grandsons, Harvey and Kenzie, with love.

'People always think I'm a millionaire because I work in television, but I'm not that rich. I have been very lucky, though.'

Fearne Cotton

Contents

Acknowledgements

During a concert performance in Las Vegas in August 1970, Elvis Presley said, 'There was a guy who said one time, he said, "You never stood in that man's shoes or saw things through his eyes, or stood and watched with helpless hands, while the heart inside you dies. So help your brother along the way, no matter where he starts, because the same God that made you, made him, too." I'd like to sing a song along the same line …' That analogy seemed apt as I readied this manuscript.

Thanks to John Blake for asking me to write it and to Mark Hanks for getting it commissioned to me. Thanks too, to my editor Vicky McGeown for being simply fantastic with every aspect of its production, and to my copy editor Jane Donovan for making sense of it all. I am also indebted to Sean Delaney at the British Film Institute for the dozens of articles and providing an accurate television listing. For their support and encouragement with most other things, my thanks go to Keith Hayward for coming up with some last-minute research facts and figures, Charlotte Rasmussen for her critique and for being such a huge fan of all my previous works ever since I wrote about Winona Ryder, Guy Buckland for the great author picture, Graeme Andrew for the stunning cover and brilliant design, Neil Rees, my Kylie cohort, for his generosity and input, John Highfield for his advice and help and for some great press, Diana Colbert for always doing such a great job with publicity, Michael Wilson for locating some late snippets of news and info, my accountant Jon Terry for, well, being my accountant, and Simon Golding for his friendship every step of the way – I cannot imagine sharing my 3am emails with anyone else. As always, my love to my children Adam and Kim for their usual enthusiasm and for understanding and appreciating the long hours that went into this work.

Nigel Goodall

Chapter 1

Meet the Family

'Growing up, there were certain things that for me encapsulated the romance of pop music. If you loved it, you'd read about your favourite bands in **Smash Hits** *or* **NME**, *save up your money to buy their records and wait all week to see them on* **TOTP**.'

Fearne Marie Cotton was fifteen years old. She had just won an audition to be a presenter for the Disney Channel in a national search for talent. Not that she had any intention of becoming a presenter; she had always had her mind set on being an actress. And that, to all intents and purposes, is the role she thought she was auditioning for. It had been her dream for the last ten years, ever since she started taking drama and ballet lessons, in and out of school. Never in a million

1

years had she thought about presenting children's shows on television.

If the secret of success is an unhappy childhood, then Fearne should never have been destined for greatness in the world of television because her childhood was everything but unhappy. There are no horror stories of abuse or lost parentage, or being moved from home to home, refuge to refuge, traumas that spiralled out of control, or being raised by druggie parents. No indeed, her story is quite the opposite. She was born on 3 September 1981 in Northwood, north-west London, but grew up in the nearby suburb of Eastcote, in Abbotsbury Gardens. From the very beginning it was quite clear that she was fortunate enough to have a pretty stable upbringing, unlike so many of Britain's most famous celebrities.

And perhaps what is more remarkable is that today Fearne is one of the most popular faces on television, both in the UK and in America, an ex-children's presenter, a rock chick with royal approval and a star. Much of her success she puts down to her mother, Lynn. 'She is exceptional,' says Fearne. 'She knew I didn't love school and wanted to do something different with my life and she didn't try and stop me. She just advised me to "do what makes you happy". If I hadn't had her support from the start, I might never have given acting and presenting a go. She's always been open-minded and supportive even in a distant way. She lets me get on with it but is interested in what I do. She's a strong woman who doesn't take any shit from anyone and definitely wears the trousers in the marriage. She's very spontaneous and impulsive.

'She'd say, "Right, we're moving house!" and we did,' Fearne recalls. 'And that's how I like to live, too. Both of her parents have passed away and I don't know how she coped, but she did. She was the one who had to break the news both times to the rest of the family, which must have been heartbreaking for her. But she helped us all to be strong. That was a massive inspiration. My mum's attitude to life is you've got to get on with it. You can't get bullied and battered in this industry and it's taught me to be strong. If you get knocked down, you get back up and carry on.

'I can't even think how I'd manage if I lost her. I just take it for granted that I can talk to her all the time – I tell her almost everything. But I know she's a massive worrier, so I hold some things back.' Her grandmother, Lynn's mother, passed away back in 2003 and Fearne still talks about her fondly: 'She was brilliant, intelligent and fun. She'd sit and chat for hours and was awful for practical jokes. She had lung cancer, endured chemotherapy and eventually died, aged sixty-eight. But the way she carried herself through was unbelievable.

'We were young kids and it was hard for her to see us being affected by it. She didn't show she was in pain and tried to make it easy for us. All her hair fell out, but she would just joke about it, saying, "I look like David Beckham, do you like it?" This was when he'd just shaved off all his hair for the first time. And she refused to wear a wig, even when we were around. She had one made but never wore it. Instead, she wore cool turbans.

'I learnt a lot about having spirit, because she never gave up or said, "It's over" – she joked until the very last day. It was her way of dealing with her illness and we got to spend time with her in a normal way. She always liked watching me on TV and I just wanted to make her proud.'

Another person she speaks of with great fondness is her Nan Ruby: 'My cousin and I take her out for a coffee once a month. When she turned eighty-five, she was still so glamorous, very "brooch matches the jacket and earrings", and looked wicked. She's blunt, too, and says the funniest things. She inspires me to speak my mind and make an effort with my appearance. When I was eighteen I dyed my hair pink and she said, "What have you done?" I was like, "Yours is bloody purple!" – she overlooked her own lilac rinse! She's also hugely up on her cultural references and watches me on TV – although she doesn't treat me any differently from her other grandchildren. She's not like some older people who live in the past. I really admire her for having a strong sense of self. She knows what she likes and has never given that up. She does what makes her feel good and thinks clothes are an important way to express yourself.'

But it is her mother who has been the biggest inspiration of all. The one thing Fearne adores most about her is how she's so calm about what she calls 'these crazy stories about me in the press'.

Behind the scenes during a photo shoot for *Cosmopolitan* magazine, the day after she attended the launch of Lily Allen's 'Lily Loves' range for high street chain New Look, she decided to spill the beans about some of those 'crazy stories'. One of them told how she apparently liked to boast about how good she was in bed: from how she wore 'naughty lingerie and high heels in the bedroom', loved sex up to four times a night, has had ten tattoos, not to mention a Brazilian wax, to how she uses her bendy figure to drive fellas wild ('I can do the splits, which is a great skill to have. I used to be a dancer so I'm very, er, flexible. I'm naturally bendy. If blokes want to explore that quality, then that's up to them.') The truth, however, is a lot less sensational: 'I did say I was confident in bed in an interview that got exaggerated. I'm not saying I'm good, I'm not saying I'm bad – I'm not saying anything!'

She had a similar experience when the gossip columns made out that she had dated more than her fair share of rocker boys and linked her to men she had never even met. 'The craziest ones were me dating Prince William and seeing the drummer [Tre Cool] of Green Day, who I think has a wife and kids. The papers just make it up.'

But yes, she conceded, 'I've dated some people in the public eye and some who aren't. It doesn't matter to me; I'm not fussy. I've got more chance of meeting someone within the business though as all I seem to do is work. If I could go on a date with any rock star, I'd go for Anthony Kiedis from the Red Hot Chilli Peppers – he's hot!' With Kiedis almost twice her age, one cannot help but wonder if Fearne perhaps prefers the older man. 'God yeah,' she sighed. 'I obviously like the more mature man. Most guys my age act like they're about twelve!'

By all accounts, the launch for Allen's 'Lily Loves' range in May 2007, two months before Fearne fronted her own range, was a bit thin on the ground when it came to Lily's celebrity friends. Most, it seemed, were absent. In fact, according to the press, it was only Fearne who was instantly recognisable when she turned out to support Allen's attempt to follow her own individual heart and tap into a different end of the fashion market, which might perhaps not have been the kind of range that some of the other big-name celebrities would want to endorse. All the same, she still managed to raise a smile as she posed with her actor–presenter father Keith Allen and modelled the floral prom-dress-style range, along with jewellery and footwear designed by the singer, which, like Fearne's own organic cotton range, was available in most high street stores across Britain.

Allen first shot to fame with her witty hit song 'Smile'

that was released to iTunes UK on 26 June 2006 ahead of the physical CD release on 3 July. It spend most of its first week at Number One on the iTunes chart before entering at Number Thirteen in the official UK Top 40. In time Lily became best known for her 'chavvy chic' style, which paired new and vintage long prom-style dresses and ball gowns with trainers and chunky gold jewellery. Although many considered she was simply acting like so many others, now following in the iconic footsteps of Kate Moss and Madonna by unveiling her own high street fashion, Allen insisted there was no rivalry.

'I don't see any point in comparing these things. I did not go into music to compare myself to other artists ... It's a bit boring, really. We are just women and trying to get on with our lives. They are both totally different women and have totally different fan bases to me. Kate Moss is a model, for God's sake, and of course they are going to sell more than I do – they are massive international names.' Despite the critical observations, she didn't see it as a competitive move on her part to challenge others such as Kate Moss, Katie Price (aka Jordan), Madonna and Kylie's more seductive and temptress range of lingerie.

If anything, Allen's 'Lily Loves' collection featured dresses that were completely different from those in the collections of the other stars. For a start, they were available in sizes ranging from 6 to 18, with high-heeled shoes, patterned trainers and floral jewellery. Allen said she had looked to the 300 dresses in her own wardrobe for inspiration and wanted something more than just the usual pretty, flowery style. She described the results as a summer collection of 'super-girly' clothes for women of all sizes. And she was probably right.

'You know how I feel about fashion: it's for everyone, not just a load of super-skinny models,' she says. The launch at 312 stores followed the shopping frenzy sparked by the Kate Moss collection that had its debut at rival fashion chain Topshop. When Moss's collection was launched, a week earlier, more than a thousand shoppers queued from noon (eight hours before the items were due to go on sale) outside Topshop's flagship Oxford Street store to get first pick of the supermodel's designs. Moss herself appeared in the window of the store wearing a long, red-neck flamingo dress from the collection.

Prices for Allen's clothes and accessories ranged from £5 for a flower ring to £55 for a 'Foxtrot Ruffle' dress. After the in-store launch, Lily changed into her favourite outfit from the collection – 'the Graffiti' dress – as she and her guests made their way to the Groucho Club in London to continue celebrations. The tabloid press were quick to notice, however, that Allen's then boyfriend, DJ Seb Chew, and her best friend, TV presenter and actress Miquita Oliver, were not present at either the launch or the after-party.

From what was noted at the party, it seemed Allen shared the same close rapport as Fearne did with her own dad. Mick, who she calls 'Mr Brightside', was not quite so impulsive a character as her mother – 'He's never raised his voice, shouted or got angry with me. He's just the calmest, nicest man on earth.' While she was growing up, he was a graphic designer, but he also worked as a signwriter for large music events such as Live Aid, and according to Fearne, he yielded to no one in his love for classic rock bands such as Led Zeppelin, The Who and The Doors – unlike her mother, Lynn, who had a penchant for Phil Spector's Wall of Sound productions, Stax and Motown. Indeed, if Fearne's mother inspired her to be spontaneous and impulsive, then it was her father who balanced his daughter's impetuous diet with music and art. In those days, years before digital downloads liberated listeners from the tyranny of instant and forgettable hits, Fearne was brought up on vinyl. It was as if this was her education rather than anything she was later to learn in school.

'I was about four when I first started to get into records. My dad would put on *Led Zeppelin IV* and play "Stairway To Heaven" over and over. I was fascinated by this gorgeous sound coming off a piece of plastic.' In 2007, she met Zeppelin's guitarist Jimmy Page: 'I met him at a gallery opening and I was a blithering wreck, saying, "I love you, I've got every album you've ever made!" I knew I had to stop or he'd think I was a loon. We ended up having a good chat, though.'

As *Rolling Stone* magazine noted, it wasn't just Led Zeppelin's thunderous volume, sledgehammer beat and edge-of-mayhem arrangements that made them the most influential and successful heavy-metal pioneer band, it was their finesse. Like the band's ancestors, The Yardbirds, they used a guitar style that drew heavily on the Blues with their early repertoire taking remakes of songs by Howlin' Wolf, Albert King and Willie Dixon, who later, incidentally, won a sizeable settlement from the band in a suit in which he alleged copyright infringement. But Jimmy Page blessed the group with a unique understanding of the guitar, and the recording studio, as electronic instruments, and of rock, as sculptural sound. Like Jimi Hendrix, Page had a reason for every bit of distortion, feedback, reverberation and out-and-out noise that he incorporated. Few of their many imitators can make the same claim and this may have been one of the reasons why Fearne loved them as much as her father did.

All the same, it wasn't until she was about seven or eight years old that her parents trusted her enough with their record player: 'After that, there was no stopping me! Whole weekends would be spent going through their collection, discovering all kinds of amazing stuff. When I was nine and getting pocket money I could afford my own records.

'I remember heading down the shops with 50p in my pocket, wondering which record would take my fancy. I happened to find a copy of the Beatles' "Strawberry Fields Forever" in a second-hand shop. It was scratched to bits but I loved it beyond words. Growing up, there were certain things that for me encapsulated the romance of pop music. If you loved it, you'd read about your favourite bands in *Smash Hits* or *NME*, save up your money to buy their records and wait all week to see them on *TOTP*.'

And of course the other fascination was the vinyl itself, she continues: 'Nothing beats the smell of fresh vinyl in the morning. It's still unbeatable as a musical format. CDs are functional but essentially unlovable and there's no magic involved in downloading a song. Playing vinyl is a beautiful ritual. What can compare to the feeling of carefully removing a treasured record from its sleeve, placing it on the deck and hearing that reassuring crackle as the needle hits the groove?

'People say "Yes, but records get scratched." I love the scratches. Some of my favourite records have scratches and those scratches become part of the listening experience. I'm not completely opposed to the iPod – I've got one and it's handy for the car. If I could play vinyl when I'm driving, I would. But flipping the records over would be a bit difficult when I'm tearing down the M1!'

When the *Mail on Sunday*'s *Live* magazine caught up

with Fearne for an August 2007 feature, she had just got back from camping with friends in Cornwall. On the second day, she confessed, 'I was craving for my fix of vinyl. So we went to a car-boot sale and picked up a load of bargains: original Elvis, Johnny Cash and Dolly Parton albums for 50p. Then I managed to find a portable, battery-powered record player going cheap in a second-hand store. We were all set up for the week – endless barbecues and music being played as it should be played. Idyllic!'

Equally blissful were the family holidays to Lulworth Cove in Dorset with her parents and her younger brother Jamie, who was born two years after her: 'We went so regularly that it became our second home and I made loads of friends there, who have stuck by me through the years despite my glitzy career. When I was fifteen, I got my first showbiz job; I found that I needed my Lulworth breaks more than ever. I was a big girl by then and went by myself for summer holidays and at Christmas and Easter.'

To this day, Lulworth Cove is still her favourite beach: 'There's a little ledge that sticks out from one of the cliff faces and hangs over the bay. My friends and I discovered it one cold Easter morning as we were walking towards the beach, so we perched ourselves down and started chatting. I think it used to be part of a wartime bunker and it became my special secret place. If I'm down there with a friend, we'll go and sit on the ledge and have a long talk. It's a great place to put other thoughts aside and just catch up.

'I haven't had enough time to visit the cove as much as I'd like to recently because I've been so busy filming and getting by on five or six hours sleep a night. But I still aim to visit at least once a year and whenever I do manage to tear myself away and drive down to Dorset in my Mini Cooper, it feels like I'm going home.

'For my 21st birthday I took eight friends to the cove. My mobile is unable to pick up a signal there, which is brilliant because it means there's nothing to do but chat and look at the fantastic view over the Channel. In the summer, the sea is really clear and the cove is as peaceful as it always was. Although I'm a coffee fiend – I got the habit after spending so much time in America [filming and travelling across the country during a road trip of a lifetime] – I love going to the teashops just inland from Lulworth, near Corfe Castle. They sell scones and have old-fashioned jars of sweets; it's like going back in time. In fact, everything about Lulworth reminds me of revisiting my childhood.'

Unlike some of the journalists to whom she has related anecdotes about her early life, Fearne balks at the stories that she was some sort of flower child, as some writers have tried to make her out to be. It was only after she became famous that she was tagged as having a hippie childhood, as if she had been raised on dandelion tea in a yurt pitched at Stonehenge. But that just isn't true, she says: 'I was born in a bungalow, we upgraded to a semi and it was just a normal suburban life. We went on camping holidays in our rubbish car and it was all very bog standard.'

True, her parents may have been slightly unconventional and the world in which they circulated may have not been typically ordinary, but that doesn't necessarily mean they are hippies. Nor does it make Fearne one, even though her mother has been variously described as a 'professional dog-walker' and a 'Tarot-reading mystic', who predicted Fearne would have three children before she turned thirty, and her father taught her to paint and encouraged her to love artists such as Edgar Degas and Paul Cézanne and Jenny Saville, famous for her portraits of curvaceous women. Lynn and Mick Cotton are probably only considered unconventional because they are passionate about what they do.

As Fearne explains, 'People always say that I make my mum out to be some kind of nutter but she's really just a very normal and interesting character. She's always meditating and practising alternative remedies and she got me into reiki [the Japanese healing technique], and she's very interested in spiritual things and guardian angels. She got me into meditating. She always told me to dream outside the box and said I could do anything if I could visualise it.'

Not only that, she continues, but, 'my mum had great style as a young woman and I take a lot of inspiration from photos of her during the seventies. As a kid, I'd always go into my mum's cupboard, dress up in this big purple silk robe and walk around the house pretending that I was a queen – so not much has changed!'

Fearne's younger brother Jamie, born two years after she arrived in the world, is quite the opposite to what one might expect. He is, she explains, 'like my dad – very shy, very chilled, doesn't say boo to a goose and doesn't give a crap what I do!' Rather than follow his sister into showbiz, Jamie chose to study for a degree in marketing. He's not at all like his sister, who from an early age loved to dress up, perform and be the centre of attention, but why should he be?

Even if Fearne had been regarded as a hippie kid on the block, there is no evidence to suggest she was an outcast or ostracised because of it. And let's face it, if you were a hippie in the early- to mid-1990s this would be a definite no-no at school. Imagine it: had she been a hippie, she would have almost certainly been considered wild, weird and anti-social at the time, and by all accounts, she was none of those things. Certainly she was never bullied or battered, either as a youngster or in her adult life, and probably the worst thing that ever happened to her at school was being called 'Fearne-tree' or 'Fearne-iture' – the nicknames the other pupils bestowed on her.

Neither did she go through the same kind of nightmare as, say, actress Winona Ryder did, who was far more of a 'hippie kid on the block' than wannabe hippie Fearne ever was. It happened when a group of fellow students decided to single Winona out on her third day in the seventh grade. Seen as an effeminate boy, the incident occurred in the hallway of her new school in between classes, when some of her fellow students decided to pounce. 'A group of guys hit me in the stomach and banged my head into a locker, so I got stitches,' Winona recalls. 'They were calling me faggot and I was like, "but wait – I am a girl!" But they didn't believe me.'

Fearne never went through such an ordeal. So, isn't it interesting to ponder that the only struggle she appears to have had to get where she is now, despite the fact that her grandfather's cousin is Sir Billy Cotton, former controller of BBC Light Entertainment – who might have made things very easy for her, but didn't – was to give up some of the things she felt she *didn't* need? One of those, she admits, was going without long student lie-ins, which she describes as 'a teeny-weeny sacrifice'.

Of course, even if she had wanted to do so, there was no real opportunity to hook up with the graduate crowd of the 1980s who were experiencing the throwback of writer and psychologist Timothy Leary's 'tune in, turn on and drop out' era. It was, after all, a decade that kicked off the 1960s' counterculture rebellion long before it was fashionable to be a societal renegade, a time when free thinking, free love and free drugs were the buzzwords of a generation.

Leary himself, of course, was a key figure of that period. Kicked out of West Point Military Academy and dismissed from Harvard as well, his adventures with hallucinogenic drugs earned him notoriety and jail time but he never repented. Even in his mid-seventies, several years before his death, he believed, 'Psychoactive brain-activating drugs are the most powerful tools humanity has for operating your mind, your brain, developing new language, building upon communications, new cultures and subcultures.'

Like a messiah attracting followers of his teachings, Leary (Winona Ryder's godfather, incidentally) was a true visionary. Bound up in those visions was the dream of change, enfranchisement and a new dawn of freedom that flavoured the 1960s even as America became more and more deeply mired in the Vietnam War.

'The long history of psychedelic drugs,' Leary taught, 'has always been associated with shamanism, mysticism, art, poetry, free sexuality, acceptance of the body, an ecological sense of the oneness of all things. This runs through Hinduism, Taoism, Buddhism, Greek humanism … There was an enormous drug influence on the French Revolution, on Wordsworth, Coleridge, Emerson, Thoreau … It's a tradition.'

It was, of course, almost ironic that early into the decade that followed, marijuana became the dope of childhood; older kids made their way through school on amphetamines, Quaaludes and liquor. But this certainly wasn't the kind of surroundings that Fearne endured as her own ambitions began to take shape.

Instead she became driven, dedicated and disciplined in all that she did and what she wanted to achieve under her own steam. Rather than worry about missing relaxations such as student lie-ins and leisure pursuits, she decided to balance her presenting jobs by studying for an A level in art at college in north-west London, where she grew up and had her first job working for her grandfather.

'He owned a flower shop and put me in charge of cleaning flower pots, a role I hated because the pots stank of rotten eggs. I worked in the shop on Saturdays and got paid about £20, which I usually spent on CDs. Granddad was quite strict and told me off quite a lot, mostly for sweeping up plants and soil in the wrong direction, which made the shop look a mess. But I could get away with being a bit cheeky and he was a joker, always having a laugh with the customers and mucking around,' she recalls.

Not so good was 'the really embarrassing photo of me, my brother Jamie and my cousin Biba when we were about six, four and two. It showed us all naked in the garden and it was placed above the shop counter. We used to beg him to take it down as all our friends walked past the shop on the way to school. But he thought it was hilarious and would point it out to my mates.

'The good things about working in the shop included hanging out with my aunt Karen and getting a lift home by car. I also got free flowers to give to my mum and learnt how to do arty stuff like arrange a lovely bunch of flowers. But I only lasted three weeks at the shop; I left after I saw an ad in the paper about a new weekend drama school – I felt it would be a better way to fill my weekends. My granddad was very understanding. I think he was glad to get a new Saturday girl who was a bit more enthusiastic!'

Compared to working in her grandfather's flower shop, school for Fearne was a similarly uninspiring experience and she grew to dislike most things about Haydon School in Northwood Hills in Eastcote village, not far from where she lived. She just didn't like it. Not that there was anything necessarily wrong with the school, but perhaps from her point of view it was simply an inconvenience compared to what she really wanted to do. And perhaps she was right when you consider that the school is now a language college, and probably nothing like it was when she attended.

All the same, like most of us at one time or another she still had her favourite teacher. His name was Mr Iggulden and he taught English, Fearne remembers: 'It's funny because English wasn't one of my favourite subjects to start with; I was really terrible at it. I was about the level of a D when I started, but Mr Iggulden got me to an A in my GCSE. I remember one specific lesson where we all went in and he brought up something quite controversial: it was something about sexism and women. He knew there were some mouthy girls in the class – especially me – and we all started to have an argument. The discussion lasted for almost the full hour and someone said, "Sir, aren't we going to do any work?" And he said, "That was your oral exam." It was a really good way to go about it – it got everyone involved.

'On top of that,' she continues, 'he was young, cool and funky. We argued a bit because I was a bit cocky but we were still friends. I always wanted to impress him, even if I did mess about a bit. I was amazed when I got my A. I was a terrible speller, but Mr Iggulden knew I was really into poetry and played to my strengths. Now I'm an avid reader – I usually have about three books on the go.

'He's an author now. He wrote a book called *The Gates of Rome* about Julius Caesar. I saw him again recently and he said, "Well done" to me for proving him wrong because he always told me I'd need my school work as a back-up in case my career didn't work out. I did drama outside school from the age of about twelve, every night and every weekend. I loved it; it was an escape from routines, which I hate. I did loads of auditions. I was working during my GCSEs and I did more and more after that. I did one A level in art. I went to the university of life and TV presenting.'

Interestingly enough, Iggulden is only ten years older than Fearne, and according to his website, he vaguely remembers half pennies and sixpences: 'I have written for as long as I can remember: poetry, short stories and novels. It's what I always wanted to do and read English at London University with writing in mind. I taught English for seven years and was Head of English at St Gregory's RC High School in London by the end of that period. I have enormous respect for those who still labour at the chalk-face. In truth, I can't find it in me to miss the grind of paperwork and initiatives. I do miss the camaraderie of the smokers' room, as well as the lessons where their faces lit up as they understood what I was wittering on about.

'My mother is Irish and from an early age she told me history as an exciting series of stories – with dates. My great-grandfather was a Seannachie, so I suppose storytelling is in the genes somewhere. My father flew in Bomber Command in WWII, then taught maths and science. Perhaps crucially, he also loved poetry and cracking good tales. Though it seems a dated idea now, I began teaching when boys were told only girls were good at English, despite the great names that must spring to mind after that statement. My father loved working with wood and equations but he also recited *Vitai Lampada* with a gleam in his eye and that matters, frankly.

'I've always loved historical fiction as a genre and cut my teeth on Hornblower and Tai-Pan, Flashman, Sharpe and Jack Aubrey. I still remember the sheer joy of reading my first Patrick O'Brian book and discovering there were nineteen more in the series. I love just about anything by David Gemmell, or Peter F. Hamilton or Wilbur Smith. I suppose the one thing that links all those is the love of a good tale.'

But not all her teachers were like Iggulden. There was one, Fearne remembers, who was very discouraging towards her and did everything he could to put her off going into the entertainment industry. She bumped into him six years after she had left school and he couldn't believe she was doing so well. 'He had to eat his words,' she recalls. 'I remember him saying at school that success in showbusiness was one chance in a million and he told me not to have high hopes about it. But I was, like, "I don't care what you say because if I have that attitude, I'll never succeed. I've *got* to think that I'm going to do it!" I had to believe in myself, so his attitude spurred me on even more. I thought, "I'm going to prove you wrong, you so-and-so." And I'm glad I did.'

But there were, of course, embarrassing moments, she

remembers, and one of those was when she and her friend Lucy went to dance school and made up routines of their own instead of doing PE as they were supposed to. They created a unique choreography for Janet Jackson's 'Together Again' and performed it wearing black tights with the crotch cut out as a top, plus lots of eyeliner. 'We thought it was brilliant,' she laughs at the memory today, admitting that in reality, 'I'm sure it was trashy as hell!'

She was passionate about going into showbusiness from a very early age; by the time she reached her teens she had attended lots of auditions and spent her evenings and weekends studying at drama school, learning tap, jazz and breakdancing, and even doing some modelling for girls' magazines like *Sugar* (which she habitually mentions to passing journalists with only the minimum of reference).

Another of Fearne's great passions while growing up was to immerse herself in books. Even though most children today would probably pick a work such as *The Lion, the Witch and the Wardrobe* or *Children of the New Forest* or *Harry Potter* as their favourite read, the most influential book of Fearne's childhood, she says, was *The Twits* by Roald Dahl: 'My mum used to read it to me. All the characters came to life but I still can't eat Heinz spaghetti for fear I'm actually eating worms!'

Equally influential, albeit for different reasons, was her

23

self-made resolution to succeed. Perhaps the teacher who was so discouraging towards her didn't realise that even as a child she was pretty determined and the philosophy she had been taught by her family was that anyone can do anything if they want it badly enough and are prepared to work hard enough for it. 'But you have to think about how to get there,' she comments. 'Just saying, "I want to be famous" isn't enough. It's got to involve thinking about what school subjects might help, how you could get a behind-the-scenes job, anything … And then, you've got to work really hard.' And that is exactly what she did. Not that she knew at first what presenting was all about. She thought 'it was just people larking about on TV – which is what I do. But as soon as I tried my hand at it, I was hooked and I wanted to pursue it seriously.'

From then on, she remembers, 'I knew what I wanted to do and I was lucky enough to go from job to job. My dream was always to work at the BBC.' With her individual look, a sort of girl gone mad in a hippie dressing-up box, she certainly wasn't the usual choice for the rather conservative Corporation, but little did she know that her dream was to ring truer than even she could have imagined.

Chapter 2

Picture Perfect

'I'm not paid to look like a supermodel – I'm paid to talk. As long as I'm doing my job and improving each week then I'd rather gauge my success on that level.'

The first time Fearne Cotton featured in the *Radio Times*, it was July 1998 and she was pictured in her school uniform. Not that that was how viewers of *Diggit* were used to seeing her; but when she wasn't presenting the Saturday morning weekend show on GMTV, she was at school revising for her most important exams: 'When I started on the show we were doing our GCSEs, but somehow we managed to find time to revise.'

Although her co-presenter Paul Ballard, known on screen as 'Des', was familiar with combining school with his television work, having spent five years working on

The Disney Club before Fearne won her audition, she herself was not so experienced. Working in television was all relatively new for her, even though, by all accounts, she didn't have any trouble mixing her educational revision with learning lines for when she was on screen. But it was, she says, a lot more difficult when the show went live: 'It was scary, because you know you've got to get it right first time and it's hard to say your lines when someone is giving you instructions in your earpiece. But it's just practice, really.'

Indeed, *Diggit* was an ideal opportunity for her to familiarise herself with the technical side of live television. It taught her how to deal with incidences such as having a voice yelling down an earpiece while she was supposed to talk directly to a camera. That alone may well have been infuriating, but her biggest problem was the early morning starts. Usually she had to be up at 4am and in the studio by 5.10am.

It probably helped that she didn't actually need that much sleep. 'As long as I've had six hours, I'm all right,' she once said. There were times, she says, when she would even go to work having had no sleep at all. And even that was okay, she continues, up to a point: 'I know that I can do it if I really have to.' But then again, she is, by her own admission, not a natural morning person, 'but I've adapted to become one because I've had to get up at ridiculous hours of the morning'. Most journalists and photographers who have worked with her agree that her best time is around midday. That is, they say, when she is really chirpy.

With or without sleep, exercise is something else that helps keep her bubbly: 'Sometimes I'll be really good and go to the gym but then when I'm working I don't always have time. I do like running, because I'm inside a studio most of the day, so it's good to get out and get some fresh air. I'm a trained dancer so I like to go to dance classes when I can as well.' Despite her slender figure, which she says she is generally happy with, this is not something she has had to work at. Neither does she have to worry too much about her diet: 'I just tend to eat when I'm hungry, although I do try to eat healthily and I am a vegetarian.'

She has been vegetarian ever since she watched a programme on live animal transportation when she was just eleven years old. That was then she decided, 'That's it, no more burgers for us, and my mum and I haven't eaten meat since. It also inspired me to get involved with animal charities.' In many ways, she says, she has Linda McCartney to thank for her decision, although she agrees that it's up to the individual whether they want to be vegetarian or not: 'For those of us who are, she helped raise awareness. I could tell from an early age that she was a good role model, a great campaigner and an amazing pioneer.'

She still admits to having cravings for the not-so-healthy goodies. One of these is Müller rice and the other is Jaffa Cakes: 'I've had cravings in the middle of the night before and have had to go to the petrol station for a Müller rice, that's how much I love them. If I'm working late, I do get really tired and a bit run-down and then I usually get a cold. It goes in phases, though. In the run-up to Christmas, I'm very busy but then I get a couple of weeks off to recover.' One of her pet hates when she does get a cold is Lemsip. According to her MySpace blog, it makes her slightly trippy, and all over the shop. 'That stuff knocks me out. I feel like my head is wrapped in a fuzzy warm blanket,' she laughs.

Fearne signed up to MySpace in November 2005, and, in the time since then she has collected a network of almost 60,000 MySpace friends, who seem to be mostly fans, although she does have a few celebrity mates in her Top 20 friends as well, such as Reggie Yates, Christopher Parker and boyfriend Jesse Jenkins. She is said to adore the idea of logging on regularly to update her blogs, blurbs, interests, music, pictures and other typical MySpace features and reading the comments that are left for her to see. 'I love MySpace,' she told *CosmoGirl* magazine in December 2006, almost a year after she first started to log on to the website. 'But there are tons of fake Fearnes on there,' she complained. One, she continues, has a 'dodgy page pretending to be me … so feel free to go on there and tell them to get lost and that they are a big fake! This is the only real page. I'm the only one who has access to it and I do check my own mails, so keep them coming, lovelies, and ignore the big old faker!' And as if to guide those who were interested to the right page, she even gave out her MySpace account number to make sure there was no confusion. The presence of fake celebrities on MySpace, however, had been steadily growing since the social networking website went live and online in 1998 and she was not alone in her concern.

In America, for instance, where MySpace was started, it wasn't long before users realised how easy it was to become 'friends' with such stars as Paris Hilton, Jenna Jameson, Hilary Duff and Madonna, to name but just a few. The profiles were real, but be warned, advised American Fox News correspondent Holly McKay, 'Your new celebrity friend may be a faux. Any Fred or Frannie, it seems, can fake stardom on the web, and sometimes even the most cyber-savvy surfers will fall for it.'

Entrepreneurs such as Bill Gates and Donald Trump, for example, have more than thirty poser profiles, while media magnets like Britney Spears and Paris Hilton appear in their hundreds. 'There are a lot of problems with predators who pretend to be celebrities,' said Parry Aftab, executive director of wiredsafety.org, a site that provides help, safety information and education to

Internet and mobile device users. 'Anybody can pretend to be anybody they want and set up a profile. MySpacers need to recognise that they are often being conned. This is illegal.'

Despite the fact that it is virtually impossible to pull the plug completely on all pseudo profiles, the big names themselves are working on the problem. In America pop star Nick Lachey isn't happy that his song, 'What's Left Of Him', is the best way to describe the multiple personalities he is meant to have, due to the vast number of varying profiles online. He is currently working with wiredsafety to establish a programme that will involve putting a stamp of certification on genuine celebrity profiles across the web world.

American celebrity Montel Williams was also shocked to discover three people claiming to be him on MySpace. 'This can be very damaging to one's career,' Aftab disclosed. 'As a father, Montel was very upset with how he was depicted on one of the pages. Another fraud page was so clever and so accurate that even he was surprised. Sometimes it can be very hard to decipher what is real and what is not.'

Unfortunately for many famous people targeted in these socialising scams, their Internet imitators can bring about real-life repercussions. San Francisco public TV host Josh Kornbluth was the prey of a pretend profile containing offensive sexual references discreetly laced throughout. In June 2007 managers at his employer, KQED, received anonymous emails from people who said they saw the profile and demanded Kornbluth be fired.

Clearly, a nasty fraud site can hurt a star. But if you think that there's no harm in setting up a site that simulates a celebrity in a supportive and non-defamatory way, think again. 'Just in getting hits on your space by pretending to be someone famous, you are benefiting commercially and that's illegal,' said Aftab. 'By all means set up a fan site, but don't pretend to actually be somebody you are not.'

So what spurs Net users to set up these bogus bios? 'Some fans do it out of flattery, not realising what they're doing is wrong,' said Australia-based media and communications specialist Stephanie Woods. 'Others want to satisfy their alter egos or experience what it may be like to lead a "better" life. As for the defamatory profiles, they usually stem from somebody who wants to vent their dislike of a particular person.'

That said, an increasing number of real celebrities are setting up in cyberspace. 'It's a way of reaching your fan base on an interpersonal level,' said Louise Kellman, a San Francisco-based PR consultant and self-confessed MySpace junkie. 'Celebrities are allowing people to get a sense of what goes on when the cameras aren't rolling. Fans really identify with that.' And when it comes to developing a drove of devotees, social networking sites seem to be working.

'People from all ages, from all walks of life, are hooked on this phenomenon and it's rising rapidly,' Kellman continued. 'So it's obvious why more and more celebs are jumping on the bandwagon. It provides them with an extra opportunity for self-promotion, the chance to stay in touch with their fanbase and of course encourages their community to participate in buying merchandise, downloading their music or going to watch their movie. Best of all, it doesn't cost a thing to set up.'

But how can ordinary fans separate the stars from the imposters? 'It's safest to always assume it's a fake,' said Jordan McAuley, founder of contactanycelebrity.com. 'Genuine profiles should always have official management contact details so you can verify their validity with them.' Aftab also advises social networkers to steer clear of anyone claiming to be a star or a close friend of a celebrity and says celebrities' publicity reps are undergoing specialist training in how to handle these hiccups. What is interesting is that while MySpace officials don't scout around for fake pages, if they receive a complaint from the victim of a falsified profile, they will immediately remove that page.

Despite the sea of scammers surfing the Net, if you understand what is real, the revolution of MySpace and other social networking sites can closely connect you with your idols and bring about a whole new family of friends. 'It's bridging the gap between the fans and the famous,' Kellman explains.

But then again, it has also become an enormous public relations accessory for many celebrities. In fact, it was once claimed that some of Lily Allen's fame was in part due to her being promoted on MySpace. In response to an interview question in which she was asked if she was discovered by MySpace, Allen argued, that no, that was 'not accurate at all! I had a record deal before I set up my MySpace account so that really couldn't be further from the truth.'

Even though she was sounding off about colds and flu and detesting Lemsip on MySpace, Fearne doesn't appear to have suffered that many colds. Well, not when she is on camera, at least, and certainly not for the year when she was presenting *Diggit*. It was a typical children's show that began in 1998 and replaced *Saturday Disney* and the Sunday morning *Disney Club*, from where Fearne got her start. The programme usually aired from 7 to 9am on Saturdays and from 8am on Sundays. Initially the programme was presented by Fearne and 'Des' and made up of Disney cartoons, old and new, plus celebrity guests, games and features. Even at its best, it was all pretty predictable fare for what one would expect from an early morning television programme for young viewers, but for Fearne there were some embarrassing moments.

One that she particularly remembers was the challenge in the forest:'There were all these quad bikers and I had to run through them and in between some cones. I was being really cocky and sprinting like Pamela Anderson down the muddy track and my foot got caught on this cone and I went flying, splat on my back. I was absolutely covered in mud.'

What was most interesting about the show, though, is how none of the other presenters, before or after Fearne, managed to get themselves a career quite like the one she now has. In fact, these days no one ever hears of them. So, whatever raw qualities she possessed, they were enough to turn her into a star while the experience did nothing of the sort for any of the others who started out on the same programme.

Not even the search launched by GMTV in September 1998 to find an additional presenter in the same way as they discovered Fearne two years earlier in a national talent hunt, most likely through an ad in the *Stage*, brought forth anyone quite like her. Once again, viewers had the chance to vote for a winner three months after the search began. The winner turned out to be Jack Stratton. For a time he joined 'Des' and Fearne to co-host both the Saturday and Sunday shows before becoming solo presenter of pre-recorded inserts for the Sunday slot. Although he left in the same year as Fearne departed from *Diggit*, the show continued to run on under the flagship of Laura Jaye and Victoria Hickson, but again, they would never enjoy the sort of success or popularity that Fearne earned for herself on the show and elsewhere.

As she would later comment, many children's TV presenters somehow sink without trace after rising from nowhere in the first place. It's similar to tinseltown Hollywood, which is littered with the corpses of child stars who one day woke to the news that they were ageing and tried to change tack before it was too late. Shirley Temple, Mickey Rooney, Margaret O'Brien, and, more recently, characters such as *Home Alone*'s Macaulay Culkin, Corey Haim from *Silver Bullet* and *Goonies*' effervescent Kerri Green were a few, although the list is endless. Even if some of them, such as Jodie Foster and Winona Ryder, continued their work on movies into maturity, their careers were never the same. It was as if the screen itself could not forgive talented precocity in actors so young. The same can be said of children's presenters, but for Fearne it was different: look back over her career and it's easy to work out why she has survived beyond the children's shows. She is upbeat, bubbly, entrancing and full of vitality. There is something very 60s and counterculture about her. And she certainly has a very different approach to presenting to any other broadcaster – it is almost 'in your face' but also quite organic and completely unique.

But not everyone thinks the same. Journalist Paul English, writing in Scotland's *Daily Record*, considered that to those over the age of fifteen, she is probably just another identikit TV presenter with a snappy line in cutesy patter, crazy dyed hair and a near-nauseating level of enthusiasm straight out of the Vernon Kay book of 'yeah' and 'whoo'-ing. But is that really the case?

In another less-than-complimentary tirade on the Internet, on *TV Scoop*, online critic and blogger Katie Button wrote that in her opinion Fearne's image seems to be her one selling point: 'Young women are supposed to like her, relate to her, want to invite her round to "ours" to eat ice cream, talk about boys and braid each others' hair. But how can she be one of us when she herself struggles to appropriately adapt her personality for her varying TV gigs? She has the kind of quirkiness that is practised and rehearsed.' It was, continued Button, 'the problem with being a female TV presenter at the moment: you perform half-decently at one gig and suddenly you're booked up until New Year's Eve 2010. There is such a dearth of proven female talent that once you hit the big time, you're everywhere. I remain rational enough to know this isn't Fearne's fault and that her career is simply benefiting from a fortuitous trend.'

In the flesh, Fearne is taller than expected: about five

foot six inches, slim and elegant, with dainty elfin features. She is everything you might expect from a Saturday morning TV presenter: fresh-faced, enthusiastic, with green eyes that are clear and bright and she always smells of a mixture of floral perfume, soap and fabric conditioner.

With no make-up and a whiff of toothpaste on her breath, she once had her hair styled similarly to Kelly Osbourne's. 'If I wasn't working in kids' TV I think I'd dye all my hair pink or try out Kelly's Mohican, but I know my bosses would probably chop my head off,' she admitted. And on the one occasion when she did have some streaks added, she was 'dead' pleased: 'I went into a punk shop in Camden and saw all these different colours, so I picked up the pink, went home and experimented. It got a bit messy and now I've got a pink bathroom!'

She has also developed a taste for outrageous clothes, something that comes across whenever she's on screen: 'I don't believe in having to match colours or styles or fabrics. I think you should wear whatever you want. I'm quite spontaneous when it comes to shopping. I don't go for the classic must-haves like little black dresses. I'll buy things that will probably only be fashionable for a couple of months but then I can pass it on to friends, a charity shop or even customise it. And I'm a big fan of customising. So if I've got something I've worn before, I'll just cut it up, stick a patch on it or paint over it so it looks different. One week I cut off one arm from a long-sleeved T-shirt and bung a stripy legwarmer in its place; I'll put anything together and see how it looks. I don't really care if people don't like my style. If it turns out wrong, at least I've had fun trying.'

It was this sort of tomboyish nature and attitude to fashion that made her stand out from other, perhaps less flamboyant presenters of Saturday morning television: 'I'm more Grunge Chick than Glamour Princess. I can't do that sexy look – I just don't feel comfortable if I wear a skirt; I'll always put a tomboy top on. Tess Daly and Cat Deeley are so glamorous, gorgeous and beautiful that I feel like the clumsy one in comparison. But I don't really think we're in some big competition or anything, we've got very different styles.'

And even when she's off-screen it's pretty much the same: she's a riot of colour. In 2003 she favoured a typical blue-and-white vest peeping out from beneath a bright pink T-shirt, a Burberry satchel, green flared cords splattered with white paint, a big, funky belt hanging off her hips and bright Converse trainers. And then another time she breezed into a north London restaurant with her blonde hair all mussed up; she was wearing clanking jewellery and had layers of floaty fabrics that appeared to be half-falling off her.

Interestingly enough, her style icon is veteran singer Debbie Harry. At first, this may seem strange when you consider that Harry's punk band Blondie were at their peak with such hits as 'Heart of Glass', 'Denis' and 'Sunday Girl' two years before Fearne even arrived into the world. And it is perhaps even stranger when you compare her musical tastes to those of her friends. 'Everything about her was so cool,' Fearne still raves to this day. 'That's why I love vintage. I got four dresses recently for £30 from a shop in Covent Garden called Wow Retro – you can't get more bargainous than that!'

Equally sacred in her personal iconography was Vivienne Westwood. Ranking her alongside Debbie Harry, she continues, 'I've been a lifelong fan of her clothes and what she stands for. She created punk as a style and a way of thinking, and still sticks by it. She doesn't follow trends but says, "This is what I'm about" and creates amazing designs. I love how she blends fashions and life; her clothes are almost political. She's a cool, strong woman and biggest showcase of how to be completely individual.

'So many young girls feel pressurised to look a certain way and she says, "Do what you want to do." I met her at the filming of the Queen's 80th birthday event. I jumped out of my skin when I saw her and staggered over, gushing at her. She was wearing a new badge she's designed: of a flying willy with sperm coming out of it. The programme producers asked her to remove it and she said, "Absolutely not!" I thought that was wicked.'

In fact, it was Westwood's approach to individuality that Fearne loved best and this was also something she picked up for herself:'I'm a bit of a fashion chameleon – I think it's good to reinvent yourself every so often. It's almost as if I have my own little fashion scene going on in my head that doesn't relate to anything else. I'll trawl around Brick Lane or Portobello Market in London for some great vintage pieces and then mix them up with the odd bit of Vivienne Westwood or Chanel. Pick and mix is what I like: a touch of something expensive with something really cheap.'

But above all else, she continues, 'I like to make a statement with what I wear. Hopefully my clothes say that I don't really care what other people think or what's going on in "celeb magazine society". The other day, for no reason at all, my friend and I turned up at a black-tie ball dressed head-to-toe as pirates. We actually looked pretty chic but it was still relatively embarrassing. We are all force-fed an ideal of what we should look like and hopefully what I wear proves that I refuse to subscribe to any of that.

'I've made loads of fashion mistakes in my time – and I still do – but I actually quite enjoy it. Recently I went to this party dressed in some mad eighties outfit: cream spotty top from a junk shop with one sleeve in lace, with this bright pink stretchy skirt, leggings, bright red boots and a massive big chain around my neck. I thought I looked really cool and like I was really expressing myself but the next week I was singled out in one of those magazines saying, "What the hell is she wearing?"

'At first I used to feel quite stung when I saw negative things about me in the press because I assumed that everyone reading it would agree but these days I really couldn't care less. If it's a personal attack about how well I'm doing my job, then that hurts, but when it's your clothes then it's just an opinion. As a society we're programmed to agree that one certain look should be "in" for a certain amount of time, which is actually just a myth created by the fashion industry. It's important that people are individual and I refuse to play that particular game.'

It's probably the reason why she launched her own 'Go Organic with Cotton' range for New Look in July 2007 that was made available in over 500 high street stores across Britain. And with a surname like Cotton, this was a marketing marriage made in heaven. The collection was aimed squarely at festival-goers and although organic menswear, baby and maternity collections were also made available, the mainstay of the range was for women.

Unlike Kylie's 'LoveKylie' collection of sexy lingerie or indeed Lily Allen's 'Lily Loves' floral prom-dress collection, Fearne's selection was far more practical with such items as denim tops, blouses, trousers, accessories and what the press called a 'gorgeous *Maribou* maxi dress' that she modelled herself, both online and out in public.

Renowned as a seasoned festival-goer, it was always going to be ideal to launch her range with a digital campaign that included her own online music, fashion and festival blog, for which Internet users could see her decked out in the entire collection, hear her views on music and fashion, as well as receive regular updates on the year's summer festivals. There were even online competitions offering such prizes as tickets to Fearne's favourite V Festival, a video iPod a day, a tent signed by the designer herself and a complete 'Go Organic with Cotton' wardrobe.

But as she herself was quick to explain, 'I'm not paid to look like a supermodel – I'm paid to talk. As long as I'm doing my job and improving each week then I'd rather gauge my success on that level. I have done a couple of magazine shoots with the "sex symbol" tag, but they take these photos when you're made up, got your hair done and you're wearing some glamorous bikini. It's not me, it's just a fantasy that they've created and I love being part of that, but it's not my reality. It's one particular image created for one particular magazine on one particular day, whereas the real me is sitting on my sofa wearing tracksuit bottoms, looking like an old hag, with unbrushed hair, eating a big bowl of cereal.

'I'm just like any other normal twenty-something: some days I wake up with a big spot on my chin, feeling a bit run-down and flabby, and other days I feel like I could take on the world. The most important thing is to walk into a room believing in yourself and in the clothes that you're wearing because if you're not comfortable, it always shows.'

Despite what blogger Katie Button posted on the *TV Scoop* website, perhaps it's Fearne's natural vivacity and quirky dress sense that got her noticed in the first place. After all, she prides herself on her boho style. She has a nose stud, tattoos and hair extensions, and refuses to be what Paul English wrote about her: 'an identikit blonde babe'. 'Oh no,' she says, horrified, 'it's important for children to see that you don't have to conform and should express yourself individually.'

For her, part of that expression lies in tattoos: 'I love working out different ways to wear my tattoos with my outfits,' she laughs. 'They're part of my style. I'm really into art, so it's an extension of that. I love getting tattoos done. I've got about ten now.' But on *Friday Night with Jonathan Ross* she told Ross that she had 11 tattoos over her body, the most notable being a fern leaf, covering her right hip up to her ribcage. Very rock'n'roll, some may think. But Fearne admits she's really not that hard-core when it comes to pain: 'One tattoo took three hours, which was horrible, but worth it in the end. I'm planning a new one now, in fact. I want something to connect the fern on my ribs and the henna plant on my back. Maybe a bit of extra foliage or something ...'

By the time she left *Diggit,* she had spent a year on the programme and was already on her way to becoming one of the most sought after presenters of children's TV. To all intents and purposes that is why she left: so that she could concentrate on other television commitments, which included such shows as *Mouse*, *Pump It Up*, *Eureka* and *Petswap.* It also meant that she could join the BBC, which of course was her dream, but the gossip columnists were also tempted to ask whether she landed a job with the Corporation simply because she was distantly related to BBC mogul Bill Cotton, son of the late wartime bandleader Billy Cotton. But, no, it wasn't how it happened, she insisted. She hadn't seen him since she was five years old and that is what she told anyone who asked; she was proud to have made it all by herself.

Before she branched out to present *Eureka*, the after-school children's science programme on CBBC, *Petswap* was probably the most popular of the shows that she was presenting on the 'other' channel. This was an afternoon weekday game show on ITV, offering animal-mad contestants the chance to change places with their pets. Ideas such as the opportunity for youngsters to run around a giant hamster wheel, store food in their cheeks and climb through an enormous cat flap were all part and parcel of the concept.

Although this was clearly a show for kids, it proved popular with both young and adult viewers. As one journalist commented, 'it was a whole lot of fun' and was superbly anchored together by Fearne, who by then was already being hailed as 'the busiest new presenter on the small screen'.

And certainly that was true. The show was another ideal vehicle for Fearne as she helped to pitch participants against each other in a series of physical and mental challenges based around a giant pet shop, a large aquarium and the *Petswap* garden. In one review the programme was described as 'Children's TV at its most mad, but brilliant stuff'. After all, where else could viewers watch contestants experience animal antics on a giant scale, from nest-building and navigation to pest problems and feeding?

According to producer Graham Brown, 'the trick was to have lots of fun doing all the things that pets do but to learn some handy tips and simple pet-care facts along the way. We wanted kids to realise that having pets is great fun but they do need a lot of care and attention as well.' This concept was something close to Fearne's own heart – after all, she did have two cats of her own. She named them Tallulah and Keloy after the magic words from Disney's 1971 *Bedknobs and Broomsticks*.

Interestingly enough, Keloy appeared in the 2006 PDSA calendar with Fearne and was photographed by the late royal photographer Lord Lichfield. With her love for animals, as far as she was concerned, it couldn't get much better!

By the time *Petswap* aired in March 2001, she had already turned her thoughts towards a place of her own: she began shopping for a property near to her parents' home and before she turned twenty she had found what she wanted. For her, moving out of the family home was particularly heart wrenching – but not for obvious reasons. How on earth would she cope with being separated from her parents' vast collection of vinyl?

'I begged them to let me to take it with me, but no luck,' she later admitted. 'They were afraid I'd throw wild parties and spill beer all over their most treasured records. They only started to relent when I got myself properly sorted in a nice, orderly flat and fixed myself up with a state-of-the-art hi-fi. Then I was allowed to borrow their collection in small instalments, solemnly promising to take care of it. Over the years I managed to borrow quite a large chunk and I've got hundreds of my own records.' Eventually, she continues, 'I also managed to persuade my mum to hand over her entire collection of original Motown singles – which I think calls for a special vinyl party at my place!'

She moved into her new flat just before she was

offered her next presenting gig, this time at the BBC for *Eureka*. Although she was thrilled about her latest challenge, she was also slightly nervous about taking it on. One of the reasons was simple: at school her least favourite subjects were science and technology, and so she thought her involvement in the show might be less successful than anything she had previously done – she was, after all, more of an arts girl. She had achieved an A grade for A level art and so the kind of shows she had been doing up to that time more or less suited her qualifications.

But as soon as she started work on the programme, she loved it: 'It showed just how exciting science is and how much fun it can be.' The part of the show that she particularly enjoyed was when she was able to demonstrate magical science experiments that viewers could also carry out at home: 'You won't believe some of the cool things which we did with vinegar on the show. We made a bone bendy by putting it in vinegar, which is pretty mad. Who would think that you could make a bone bendy? We even showed how to make an egg bounce using vinegar!'

She was also convinced that her favourite 'High Tech Eureka' featured on the programme was going to become a real craze. 'We show amazing new sweets for the first time on British TV, which have holograms stamped onto the surface. They look unbelievable,' she enthused at the time. 'I reckon they'll be a huge hit. We also made a hologram in the studio using a laser pointer, which was absolutely incredible. It looked so beautiful.'

This time around, she shared presenting duties with Kate Heavenor, who had landed her first presenting job on another CBBC show, *Fully Booked*. Since then, she had presented *Hyperlinks* and *FBi*, and had fronted *The Crew Room* on BBC Choice as well as appearing on *Children In Need*, a programme that Fearne would later end up being involved with herself.

Like Fearne, Kate had no formal science training to be a presenter for a science and technology programme for kids but she did have a scientific father of sorts, who became an accomplished inventor. A dentist by trade, he identified a need for a toothbrush that would encourage people to hold the brush at a 45-degree angle and developed a brand of handle that is successful in helping to hold awkward or heavy objects easily. It's now used on a diverse range of products, from saucepans to baby buggies.

Looking back, Kate has particularly fond memories of recording the 'Wild Eureka' part of the show that looked at the part science plays in the animal kingdom. In one item she filmed about pelicans, the pelican in the studio somewhat unexpectedly decided to use Kate's head as a convenient perch. She even got a kiss from a sea lion: 'I knew that if I just gave the sea lion a peck on the cheek it would turn away really quickly and we wouldn't get the shot we needed. So I really went for it and gave the sea lion a smacker on the lips! Fearne couldn't believe what I'd done and she still makes fun of me for it.'

In another programme, Kate and Fearne explained how a tornado works, thanks to a large demonstration machine set up in the studio. Kate found herself spinning round and round on a large disc to demonstrate how things at the centre of a tornado move much faster than they do nearer to the outside: 'We recorded the item straight after lunch and we had to do it quite a few times. At one point I felt very queasy because of all the spinning. I'm sure I looked quite ill on the finished programme.'

When they weren't working together, Kate and Fearne would spend their time off-camera hanging out with each other, doing what most girlfriends do. Then a regular visitor to Fearne's new flat, Kate was always popping round for what she called a natter: 'I've even got my own special box of tea there so I don't drink all of Fearne's. I haven't got a toothbrush there yet, but let's just say that our clothes have become rather interchangeable.'

Chapter 3

The Big One

'I'm a sad granny who stays in my house with my cats. I don't go out on a Friday because I'd be too tired, and I really have to be on the ball on a Saturday morning.'

It had become one of the most popular programmes on Saturday morning television and introduced viewers to some of Britain's best-loved presenters, including Emma Forbes, Andi Peters, Zoë Ball, Jamie Theakston and Katy Hill, but eight years and eight series later, *Live and Kicking* had run out of steam – and viewers. So when it was announced in September 2001 that *The Saturday Show* would take its place, with a completely new approach, it was hoped this would be exactly what was needed to get the BBC back into the

Saturday morning ratings. Described as the ultimate participation show, already it was being branded as cheeky, rude, loud and very risky before anybody had even had a chance to see it.

According to the advance information, it promised to be a radical departure from the more conventional Saturday morning show that the viewers were used to. But somehow it didn't quite deliver its promise. Well, not to start with at any rate. One of the first problems, it seemed, was the curious choice of Dani Behr as one of its two presenters, to which the critical objections grew louder and louder as the series rolled on.

Although she first came to prominence, quite controversially, on Channel 4's *The Word*, Behr actually became more famous for what she did off-camera rather than anything she accomplished in front of it. In fact, it was when she announced to a British lads' magazine that she'd had 'seedy but great sex in a car park' that the BBC decided to axe her from *The Saturday Show* just six months after she started.

Although *The Word* was originally broadcast at the 6pm time slot recently vacated by *The Tube* on Friday evenings, it was soon shifted to a late night 'post-pub' slot to continue its live magazine format of interviews, live music, features and even adult-themed games. The flexible late night airing also meant that guests could do just about anything to be controversial. There was an 'I'll Do

Anything To Be On Television' section called 'The Hopefuls', in which people ate worms, bathed in maggots and generally did repulsive things just to be featured. For its time, the show was considered to have pushed forward the boundaries of youth television programming, and it turned Behr from a more or less unknown into a TV star.

Not that it helped matters that the tabloid press busied themselves with revelations of her flings with a string of footballers and a boy band star. Even though the BBC requested her not to talk publicly about her colourful love life, she apparently still did. She also boasted about how she intended to make *The Saturday Show*: 'better, sassier, sexier and more stylish'. Maybe, but she was still deemed unsuitable for a children's programme. As one critic pointed out, 'Dani's always looked like she just got out of bed after a big night out.' Others branded her cold and wooden: 'Children like to believe presenters are their pals but Dani came across as too much of a dominatrix!'

Not that online reviewer Steve Williams was totally convinced. Sure, she may have been seen as an odd choice and her CV was hardly that of a children's presenter, but she wasn't as bad as some might think, he claimed. In fact, 'she seemed to relate to the audience quite well and she wasn't averse to doing a silly dance or putting on a stupid costume when the need arose.'

All the same, she left the programme at the same time as her co-presenter, Joe Mace, whose contract wasn't renewed either. The show then moved from Studio 6 at Television Centre and returned to its traditional summer home of Glasgow. Fearne was recruited to take over from Dani Behr, and Simon Grant (at the time a total unknown) became her co-presenter.

Interestingly enough, Grant had been working as an entertainment rep for a holiday company and spent the previous two and a half years at family hotels in the Balearic and Canary Islands performing in front of audiences. He sent out literally thousands of letters to every television and radio network that he could think of. After all, he had the perfect grounding to make it work, or so he thought. But never in a million years did he think that he would ever end up working for the BBC. Although he had sent them his show reel some time before, when they actually called him he was taken by surprise. But as soon as he answered the phone, he recalls: 'They said, "Come in for an interview." I had a screen test and then I had about eight interviews after that – I even had to dress up as a pirate! With acting and presenting, you just need to open all the doors.'

With some major tweaking to the format of the show that included a few new features to replace the ones that hadn't worked first time round, once again there were high hopes for success. There was a new 'liquid sunshine' set that replaced the three-tier one that, according to Grant, was 'very bright and early morning'. A new logo –

a bit Austin Powers, swirly and 70s style – was also created. But at 11.15am, it would all change into a glitzy stage for another of the new features to be introduced: a Saturday morning edition of *Top of the Pops*.

TOTP was the longest-running music show on UK television and as so many of the other Saturday morning shows then included music segments of their own, why not have one on *The Saturday Show*? After all, the success of the ITV Saturday shows such as *SM:tv Live* and *CD:UK* had led to the axing of *Live and Kicking* in the first place. Not only that but the launch of *Top of the Pops Saturday* would hopefully grab back some of the viewers who had switched over to the ITV channels. The idea was to package together performances from the Friday evening show, along with new footage, interviews and live acts as well as to go behind the scenes.

When Fearne's manager, Amanda Astall, told her the news, she was over the moon about being the new presenter. In the week leading up to the announcement of the new show and having spent the previous few months rehearsing and developing ideas with Grant, Fearne admitted, 'I probably won't sleep on Friday night. It doesn't feel like Saturday is ever going to come. This has been the longest week of my life!' She was excited because, first and foremost, her greatest love is music. It's something that comes across at every one of her live gigs, even when she's slightly tipsy, as she was when she was filmed doing a set in the Font at the University of Hertfordshire by a student who was in pretty much the same condition and to this day she wonders how on earth she held up her camera for so long.

Astall understood her love of music as well, and that is why Fearne says she totally takes advantage of her manager: 'I speak to her six times a day and she's there no matter what, even at midnight! I'm quite scatty and she's on top of everything; she has a memory like an elephant – she looks after me *and* Ant and Dec. She's like the Bionic Woman!

'And she's rescued me loads of times, booking cabs for me when I've been stuck somewhere after a night out,' she continues. 'She's honest and open, too. Although it's a work relationship, we look out for each other as friends, which means she has her say on my boyfriends. I have a lot of drinks with management and we even go on holiday together, so it's important that boyfriends fit into that family. There have been a few guys – okay, *quite* a few guys – where's she said, "Er, not great!" If I haven't got a job or I'm not sure about a particular one, she tells me to remember it's not about the money, it's about happiness.'

And happiness is the word that best describes how excited she was about the prospect of *Top of the Pops* becoming an essential part of Saturday morning viewing because the experience would also give her the opportunity to meet some of her idols. Despite what was being said, she insisted: 'We're not copying *CD:UK*. *TOTP* is already such a well-known brand that it has given us respect. People believe it will be a cool show. And we're going to bring *TOTP* to a different audience from the ones who don't miss it every Friday night. It also gives us the chance to get some great bands on.'

She was also thrilled that *The Saturday Show* had switched production to BBC Scotland: 'I'm really looking forward to getting out and about in Glasgow for the shopping and the nightlife.' She laughed at the thought: 'I reckon I could single-handedly boost the city's economy.' Not that she was going to find the time to do any of that. She is probably one of the few twenty-somethings happy to sacrifice her hallowed playtime for work, but this is something she willingly does.

'I don't go out ever, actually,' she stated, with an honest realisation. 'I'm a sad granny who stays in my house with my cats. I don't go out on a Friday because I'd be too tired, and I really have to be on the ball on a Saturday morning. It's a three-hour live show and I have to be aware of what I'm doing the whole time. There's no autocue so I can't afford to be at work with a hangover. It's the same on Sundays when I present *Smile*. I'm a perfectionist; I'm desperate to make what I do brilliant. The show is aimed at the young teenage market and much of what they like comes down to image rather than vocal talent and instruments.'

This was certainly true. As journalist Cath Bennett correctly noted, 'Saturday morning telly is great for easing yourself through a hangover and keeping the kids quiet for a precious few hours. The soothing mix of cartoons, silly games, celeb chat and music is the perfect way to kick-start the weekend. For the people who create such easy viewing, Saturday morning heralds a stress-fest, and the climax of their working week.'

Writing in the *Daily Record* of going behind the scenes in June 2003, Bennett was surprised to find out exactly what was involved in creating the programme. Arriving bleary-eyed just before 9am, she came across a hub of excited people bursting with anticipation as they prepared to go on air. Tripping over dancers warming up, make-up artists wielding their brushes and rows of kids being herded into place, she made her way on to the set: 'As sound engineers did their final checks, the audience – perfectly groomed ten- to seventeen-year-olds – were warmed up. This involved practising dance moves, waving their arms, and cheering and laughing as loud as they could. At 8.59 a final layer of lippy was applied to Fearne Cotton, and then it was showtime.'

Composing themselves for the camera, Fearne and Simon introduced the show and their main guests for the day: Dannii Minogue and Delta Goodrem. Surprisingly, they both do all this from memory without the aid of an autocue. As Fearne explained, 'We rehearse the show on a Thursday and have pointers about what we are going to say but there is no real script. Basically, we just have to be really on the ball and say what comes naturally. This does mean we can't go out and get really drunk on Friday nights. You couldn't do this job with a hangover.'

Even saying what comes naturally can be quite a challenge, though. Both presenters have an earpiece, through which producers yell instructions to speed up, talk up or wind up. The entire crew are guided by an intricate timetable itemising every second of the show and this has to be followed with military precision.

'If a guest carries on talking for too long you have to try and wind it up without it all seeming too contrived,' Simon continues. 'Because the whole thing goes out live there is a risk. We were a bit worried about Kelly Osbourne when she came on. But the guests do have prompts for certain parts of the show.' Indeed, the prompts come in the form of hastily written placards brandished by harassed floor staff. 'You can only do so much in our rehearsals before we go out live,' he went on to say. But as Fearne revealed, 'It can be really funny because you end up with some big hairy member of the crew pretending to be Dannii Minogue so we can practise!'

The fascinating thing about the BBC Scotland studio, observed Bennett, was just how tiny it was: 'On the telly it looks like there are many different areas used for the singing, the games and the cosy chats, but the show is actually filmed in a space less than half the size of a football pitch and the crew have to be incredibly organised to keep everything running smoothly. Corridors are filled with psychedelic backdrops and luminous sofas, and I nearly tripped over a large bucket of green gunge, which I learnt was used in the Pick Your Nose game.

'With my access-all-areas pass, I was able to go right into celeb-spotting heaven, the corridor where the guests have their dressing rooms. In proportion with the studio, these too were incredibly small, each containing just a sofa, dressing table and rails on which to hang clothes. The dressing rooms revealed a lot about the celebs residing in them. Sneakily opening a closed door, I discovered singer Jamelia in a clutter-free haven having her make-up applied.

'The real noise was coming from the end of the corridor and a room where music was blasting while glamorous people ran to and fro. Peering in, I found Dannii Minogue sucking on a lollipop, surrounded by a muddle of clothes, make-up and squashed chocolate. "These lollies are fantastic," she confessed. "A friend of mine who lives in Paris invented them for me. Once you've finished them, you find a glow-stick inside." Dannii was constantly on set during the morning, rarely having more than ten minutes to herself throughout the three-hour programme. "I love doing this show and I always have a really good laugh with Fearne. Probably my favourite part today was the height game, where the kids have to work out who is tallest. That's really good fun."'

Someone else who enjoyed the Play Your Heights Right game was eleven-year-old Greg McLouchlan, who was plucked from the audience to take part in the competition. He won a stash of prizes, including a digital camera and one of Dannii's magic lollies; he couldn't believe it: 'It's been brilliant being in the show. It's great to get so close to all the stars. I think my friends will be really jealous when I go to school on Monday.'

Escaping the organised chaos of the studio, Bennett found her way to the real nucleus of the show – the gallery: 'Surrounded by television screens, clocks and a desk full of switches, producers and directors carefully create the pictures we see on our screens. In an atmosphere bursting with pent-up intensity, they count through every second of the show and carefully merge the live action with previously recorded footage and cartoons.'

At 11.15am Bennett watched in amazement how it was all change as *The Saturday Show* turned into *Top of the Pops Saturday*: 'The familiar white-and-black screens replaced the multi-coloured backdrops and crew scurried around clearing up crisp packets and gunge, remnants of the morning's games.'

After a busy morning the guests geared up for their final appearances. Delta, better known as Nina on *Neighbours*, was bubbling with excitement and admitted: 'This is just so much fun. We don't really have morning shows like this in Australia, but I love doing them.'

By midday the show was in the bag and everyone heaved a sigh of relief. 'I just can't eat on Saturday mornings,' confessed Simon, collapsing into a squishy sofa. 'But once the show is over I have to go and get myself a big burger.'

In the end, Fearne and Simon agreed that filming had gone well, allowing for the usual collection of hiccups. Fearne giggled, 'I had a dress on in this game we were playing and it fell down, Judy Finnigan style.' Simon admitted, too, that he had forgotten his lines: 'It was just after the S-Club 8 karaoke and I was so shocked at how good the kids were, I forgot what I was meant to say next.'

It's not difficult to work out how much the presenters, who laugh and joke as much away from the screen as on, enjoyed their jobs – especially Fearne: 'It's just so different every week, and you get to meet so many interesting people – I love it.' The show over, there was a sense of togetherness as presenters, guests and audience members mingled, hugged and wished each other luck. The crew were slightly more pragmatic and carefully packed up the set, aware that in next to no time they'd be doing it all over again.

In between, Fearne would take the opportunity to catch up with some of her own favourite music. Although she openly admits that Justin Timberlake, the White Stripes, Coldplay and the Hives were at the top of her CD pile at the time, 'I really like mellow stuff too, like Beth Orton, Jewel and Tracy Chapman. The last CD I bought was Carole King's *Tapestry* …' (which beggared belief among some journalists). Who would have thought that a petite pop presenter would listen to a seminal acoustic masterpiece over thirty years old? Well, Fearne does!

Even if it might perhaps now be considered a little restrained for someone of Fearne's age, one cannot help but picture her on a Friday night with her cats listening to Carole King singing 'You've Got a Friend'. 'Oh no, please don't paint that image!' she laughs. Although she says that Mondays and Tuesdays were her weekends, her friends were away at university all over the place and so her weekday 'weekends' were usually spent with student boyfriend Tom, the relationship with whom she refused to elaborate on. Neither did the tabloid press. Or at least, they didn't back then. She was also pleased that none of the so-called lads' magazines had come knocking on her door for any kind of gossip. Even today she has yet to face the same kind of questioning which led to the demise of her *Saturday Show* predecessor.

Fearne, however, considers that wasn't the only reason. Not one to spill the beans, she was keeping quiet about whatever she thought about the programme. As she confirms, 'they wanted the show to be more kid-related'. And that is what they ended up with. It must have also helped that there was no dirt to dish up on her. Despite this, she had to admit that she was less than enthralled when she had to pose for pictures with *Fame Academy* winner David Sneddon to publicise his presenting stint on the show for two weeks in July 2003. As photographers asked the couple to cosy up a bit more, the usually mild-mannered singer told her to 'get her tits out!' Fearne couldn't believe it. This was one of the few times when she felt totally embarrassed. But about thirty seconds later, David apologised to her and they got on with the shoot.

All the same, there was still the odd bit of gossip about her doing the rounds. One of those times was when it was reported that she had apparently been spotted kissing Chris Parker, who was at that time playing Shane Ritchie's son, Spencer Moon, in the BBC soap *EastEnders*. He was then receiving 2,000 fan letters a week and had already earned himself a reputation for being a red-hot lover off-screen; already he was at the centre of a kiss-and-tell in one of the Sunday tabloids. His former girlfriend Lucie Clark, who described him as a 'superstud', talked of their four-times-a-night sex romps and how he made love to her all over his house in Hampstead, north London. But instead of hitting the roof, Chris decided to look on the funny side: 'My friends read it and just said, "Your kitchen's not big enough for that!"'

But in the case of the Chris and Fearne story, it really was a case of the wrong girl. And certainly he wasn't kissing her behind Lucie's back. In fact, he wasn't kissing her at all! Again he saw the funny side to the situation. What happened, he explained, was 'I'd met a girl called Holly Willoughby at a *Top of the Pops*' party and we'd gone to this club afterwards. After a few more drinks Holly and I snogged on the dance floor. We were really tonguing each other and the next day someone put two and two together and got five, saying it was me and Fearne. It didn't mean anything. Holly and I are good friends. It was just one of those things you do when you're drunk.'

As he pointed out, his hectic filming schedule meant a serious girlfriend was out of the question, so all in all, this was just a bit of fun. Besides, 'It's hard for a girl when you have to say you haven't got time to see her. Sometimes I don't want to go home and share my bed with anyone. I want to get in, cook myself something healthy, learn my lines and go to bed at half nine so I can get up at five.'

Much the same as it must have been for Fearne when

her time was at such a premium. Not only did she have *The Saturday Show* to think about, she was also presenting *Smile* and *Finger Tips* (an arts and crafts programme for children), and had just started on *Record Breakers*, an experience that was sometimes scary, she recalls. One of those times was when 'the producers asked me if I'd like to abseil down the main tower at Canary Wharf in London. Obviously I said, "No, not really" but I got persuaded to do it. I was terrified. The building is 800 feet high, but I had a hunky marine called Dean encouraging me, which helped. We broke the record for the most people to abseil a freestanding building within an hour but I nearly passed out afterwards. I was like, "Take me to the pub!" It was only 11am but I needed a vodka.'

Not that this was quite so terrifying as the moment when fellow presenter Davina McCall half-scared herself to death on *Don't Try This At Home*. In fact, at the time, it was probably considered to be one of the most terrifying moments on television: Davina had to bungee-jump 700 feet out of a helicopter over the Grand Canyon in Arizona. No question about it, 'the worst thing I have ever done in my whole life,' she recalls today. 'I cried every day for a week. I'd wake up in the mornings and go to sleep at night with nothing but that experience on my mind.'

The daredevil stunt started when careworker Jason's

girlfriend, Rebecca, wrote in to the show saying that Jason (who had already done a crane bungee jump) boasted no challenge was too scary for him. However, 'curiosity killed me when I looked out into that abyss and I thought, "No way!" I asked the stunt guy to push me, but he said he couldn't. My own body wouldn't allow me; I was glued to the spot. So we came down and poor Davina had to do it instead.'

Not so scary was Fearne and Holly Willoughby's friendship. They had been good friends with each other for ages and they are still great buddies to this day. It's easy to see how the mistaken identity of the girl Chris was kissing on the dance floor occurred as Fearne and Holly are also very much alike in terms of looks, shape and height. But that didn't stop the gossip columns suggesting there was more to it when Fearne and Chris went camping to the celeb-studded V Festival about a year later.

'V' was one of Britain's first annual music festivals to be held simultaneously at two different sites, one at Hylands Park in Chelmsford and the other at Stafford's Weston Park. Originally, it seemed only appropriate that the year the festival took place should be added after the 'V', but since 2003, the date has been dropped.

The northern leg of the first event in 1996 was held in Warrington, moving to Temple Newsam, Leeds, for V97 and V98, and then moving again in 1999 to its current home at Weston Park, Stafford. Interestingly enough, the 'V' represents the Virgin Group and the whole idea behind it was simply to promote Richard Branson's companies – the events have continued to be sponsored by Virgin Mobile, always with Virgin Radio as the official radio station.

Although the festival generally takes place during the penultimate weekend of August, certain critics have long disliked its corporate sponsorship and reputation for being the most elite of the major British music festivals that include Reading and Leeds. However, the weekend format, low queuing times and professional organisation have all given the event a loyal audience that has resulted in record sell-outs.

Although predominantly rock, the festival books a wide range of music and is probably the most likely among the festivals in Britain to book pop names such as Mel C, Dido, Nerd, Razorlight and Faithless. Indeed, over the years V has showcased a mixture of British and international musicians from up-and-coming bands such as Coldplay and the Kaiser Chiefs, glam rockers El Presidente to veteran crooners like Tony Christie, Girls Aloud and McFly.

It was during the V Festival, when Fearne and Chris attended to enjoy the bands playing there, that one of those ubiquitous 'friends' (who always seem to be on hand to comment about matters of the heart) revealed that Fearne had sent Chris into a spin after they shared a tent together. But it seemed there was nothing in it: 'Chris is a brill guy but they are just good mates. Fearne doesn't want anything more than that.' Besides, it wasn't long before the camping weekend that she had apparently 'pulled' Lostprophets frontman Ian Watkins at the *Kerrang!* Awards: 'Ian is definitely more her type. He has that rock star rebel image.'

Not only that, but Fearne was also being linked to Green Day drummer Tre Cool. The US punk-pop band appeared on *Top of the Pops* in December 2004 with their hit of the time, 'Basket Case', when Fearne was co-presenting the show with a different guest presenter each week. But that is not where she met him. It was not until the American band played the first of two nights at London's Brixton Academy the following month that she had the chance to hook up with him and the rest of the band.

After the gig, she joined the boys for a few after-show drinks and that is apparently where Cool made a beeline for her. According to the *Mirror*'s source, they really hit it off: 'Fearne and Tre were chatting and laughing all night. At the end of the evening they swapped numbers and the next day they went shopping together on Bond Street. Cool had to dash off for a sound check but he sent Fearne a text saying, "I've taken the liberty of putting you on the list for tonight".

'But she couldn't make the show even though Cool was asking after her all night. So instead, they planned to hook up again at Green Day's Milton Keynes Bowl concert.' Fearne did her best to shrug off all the attention from the tabloids. After all, she reasoned, she and Ian were only sort of dating, rather than anything serious, so in her mind it was okay to go out with someone else. She was simply talking about meeting up at a gig and surely there was nothing wrong with that?

In the end, the event was awesome, she says, the best Saturday night out she's ever had: 'I went with loads of mates on a big coach. It was boiling, and we all danced and jumped around while the sun set. I got on my mate's shoulders and a security guard told me off, much to my embarrassment. We all stopped off for pies and crisps on the way home at about one in the morning. The garage couldn't believe their luck – we wiped them clean out of food!'

Hardly the stuff of headline news … Not that it mattered anyway for it was never going to be the type of headline that would turn Fearne into a tabloid favourite like when she went public about her relationship with Peter Brame. Like Kate Moss and Pete Doherty, this was a relationship made in tabloid heaven: Fearne was young, sweet and charming while Brame was a hell-raising party monster. The gossip columnists couldn't go wrong …

Chapter 4

Stairway to Fame

'I've met Kylie lots of times and I both love and detest interviewing her. She's the most lovely lady but I feel like a big farmer's wife next to her. She's this petite, gorgeous creature, like a sculpture.'

In February 2003 and one week before Valentine's Day, the most romantic date of any lovers' calendar, Fearne joined Ulrika Jonsson, John Thomson, Will Mellor, Jo Brand, Paul Ross, Ruby Wax, Doon Mackichen and Kwame Kwei-Armah to head over to Witanhurst Manor in London's Highgate, where the *Fame Academy* was housed, to start the boot-camp training needed for a special celebrity version of the show that would raise money towards Red Nose Day for Comic Relief.

In the two weeks that followed, she and her fellow celebrities were placed at the mercy of teachers, voice coaches, keep-fit experts, and finally, the viewers, who would vote whichever candidate they considered not good enough off the programme during its week-long run. Once installed in the house, she and her colleagues were subjected to arduous sessions in the dance studios, the rehearsal rooms and later, of course, in the limelight. The head teacher was once again Richard Park, who had assembled more or less the same team behind him as for the first non-celebrity series the previous October: vocal coaches Carrie and David Grant, choreographer Kevin Adams, personal tutor Jeremy Milnes and music coach Jo Noel.

In the week before the show went live, each day a host of celebrity experts dropped into the house to offer their own tips on how to be successful in the challenge that Fearne and the others were now almost ready to take on. Andrew Lloyd Webber guided her through a group performance, England rugby star Laurence Dallaglio tested her fitness levels, hypnotist Paul McKenna helped her to overcome any stage fright and celebrity hairstylist Nicky Clarke gave her a makeover.

Although the show was never intended to discover a new singing talent, it did aim to raise money for Comic Relief. In fact, every time viewers voted to save their favourite celebrity student, the charity received cash that would help to bring about an end to poverty and social injustice in the UK and Africa.

Like the original format of *Fame Academy* broadcast six months earlier, the celebrity version was run along the same lines. Although it was still pretty similar to *Pop Idol* and *Popstars* that had gone before it, *Fame Academy* went one step further. It was the first programme to introduce a relatively new approach that was much more than just another talent contest, with contestants singing on weekly live shows as they had done ever since Hughie Green's *Opportunity Knocks* graced the small screen in the 1960s.

If nothing else, *Fame Academy* could claim to be a talent show that encouraged its contestants to write their own songs and music as well as to develop individual performer's singing techniques and performing skills. For a period of ten weeks, the students were given a complete musical education that included one-to-one vocal coaching, songwriting lessons, personal development, fitness/dancing classes and workshops with professionals. They were provided with dormitory-style living accommodation, communal meals and recreation areas in much the same way as the celebrities who appeared in the Comic Relief edition.

In many ways, this was the first reality TV talent show. Like *Big Brother*, the students were completely cut off from the outside world and not allowed to leave the

Academy without supervision. They were also constantly televised through a vast network of cameras monitored twenty-four hours a day so that viewers could watch their every move, from when they woke up in the morning until the time they went to sleep. It was like having all-areas access to what went on behind the scenes. Singing lessons, dance classes, rehearsals and costume fittings were all captured on camera, as well as daily routines such as meal times, relaxation periods and private moments. Certainly, the social interactions between the students and the growing tensions as their numbers dwindled all added to the interest of the show, day by day and week by week.

The basic idea was to put a dozen or so aspiring young people in a house, expose them to top-quality musical tuition, have them perform on national television, remove one of the weakest performers each week, then ultimately whoever is the most popular person in the final week becomes the winner. *Pop Idol* had already aired one successful series, so anything *Fame Academy* brought to the table would be judged against *Pop Idol* judge and creator Simon Cowell's show. Following an unusually large media exposure of hype, the first series was launched with glitz, glamour, high hopes and a contest to vote a final person into the Academy. But the show fell flat on its face with a so-called 'gala opening' that was full of missed cues, bad dancing and lots of out-of-tune singing. Even worse was when one of the original contestants strained her voice so badly that she was forced to withdraw and the runner-up in the opening show gained a late readmission.

Although it was an amazingly poor start that had many critics – and even the general viewing public – wondering, it helped conceal many of the show's weaknesses. Adding to the misery, though, was the complex elimination procedure in which competitors were evicted. It worked by having three of the worst performers each week nominated by Richard Park, with assistance from vocal coach Carrie Grant and fitness instructor Jeremy Milnes. Then public voting by telephone started on the Monday and the lines closed towards the end of the Friday night live show.

Whichever contestant had the most phone votes was safe from elimination. The remaining two were forced to face their fellow contestants, who would decide to keep one of them and eject the other. What is perhaps interesting is how the balance of power shifted as the series rolled on. In the early weeks, Richard Park's prejudices counted strongly but as the number of contestants decreased, the public and internal vote became all the more powerful.

Despite a weak format and a studio set that was cold and uninviting, in its final weeks the first series of *Fame Academy* finally blossomed into a show worth watching, in much the same way as the celebrity version of Comic Relief. The biggest change came in the elimination process. Out went the concept of Richard Park nominating three contestants for the public vote and in came a perpetual all-up vote. The bottom three in the public vote would then face the judgement of Park plus the others and their favourite performer would be safe from elimination. The last two were then judged by their peers, with the performer achieving the lowest score being asked to leave the show.

Fearne left the celebrity version on the second night after she performed her version of Travis's 'Driftwood'. It was pretty clear from her performance that she would get voted off. In fact, Park branded her singing like, 'a third-year high-school class concert performance'. He told her to stick with what she did best: being a children's presenter.

She agreed totally: 'I was dreadful! I can't blame anybody for voting me out – I deserved it. I couldn't sing but at least I tried. I still get people coming up to me in the street, impersonating my dreadful version of "Driftwood".' Even today she openly admits that her out-of-tune rendition was appalling: 'I would have made the same decision if I had been watching; I was poor.'

After she had been voted off the show, she remembers she must have looked like some kind of deranged pixie – or at least that's what she thought sometime later when a journalist showed her a picture of the moment: 'I left the building to find this Christopher Biggins character on a motorbike, telling me to hop on. I hadn't been in the public eye that much before *Fame Academy* and it was a mad, crazy time. Singing isn't really my forte but I knew it would be something to tell the grandkids about. It was extraordinary waking up in the morning, thinking, "Oh, there's Ulrika Jonsson next to me and there's Ruby Wax over there." So surreal! All I wanted to do that night was go home with my mum and dad, have fish and chips and get back to normality.'

Ultimately, actor Will Mellor was crowned the winner, beating comedienne Ruby Wax to the post. In the grand finale, live from BBC Television Centre, Cat Deeley and Patrick Kielty arrived on stage after a warm introduction from hosts Ant and Dec as all eight celebrity contestants were brought back. The finalists, Will and Ruby, both made one last live performance. Voting lines closed when the main Comic Relief show came on air, the public vote was counted and the result announced after 9pm. An emotional Mellor thanked everyone who had voted for him, as Cat welcomed actor Hugh Grant to the stage to present Will with his kitsch winner's trophy, and Ruby with a CD of her unique singing from the week of live shows. Doon, Kwame, Will, Jo Brand and Ruby all returned to the stage later that evening, well after midnight, to dish the dirt on what really went on in the

Academy in an interview with Graham Norton. Although there had been much criticism and many bad reviews, this was still the biggest hit the BBC had had in years.

Back in the normality that she had begun to crave, Fearne was forced to admit, 'If truth be told, my mates won't even let me do karaoke any more. They reckon my version of "Killing Me Softly" was more like "Killing Me Very, Very Slowly"! Even my cats seem to object if they hear me singing in the shower. I swear I can hear them shouting, "Oooh, Mum, no more, please. Leave us in peace!" So I don't think I'll be asking for a record contract just yet.'

In many ways, it was perhaps slightly surprising that she agreed to make an appearance in the first place. It probably didn't help that Richard Park wasn't the only one who didn't think she was brilliant. In fact, many thought she was there just to be the 'totty' of the show. But, as most of her critics acknowledged, not even her cutesy blonde image and skimpy clothes could compensate for the fact that she was unable to sing. And had it not been for the arrogance of presenter Paul Ross (elder brother of Jonathan), she would have probably gone home first: 'She was that bad.'

All the same, she still insisted her singing aspirations were not completely dispelled, no matter what everyone was saying or thinking about her vocal talents. If anything, she jokes, she was thinking of setting herself up for a new career as a celebrity wedding singer despite what had been described as caterwauling her way through Fran Healy's hit and mauling Roberta Flack's soul classic 'Killing Me Softly' the night before she 'murdered' Travis's 'Driftwood'.

Despite the fact that there were those who were surprised that she took it on, she was glad that she had, even though headmaster Richard Park wasn't exactly to her liking: 'It was great fun to be working with Ruby and Jo; having breakfast and getting dressed with people I'd grown up watching on TV was quite an experience.' But Richard Park was a definite no-no: 'I didn't like him. He really crushed me in rehearsals, told me I sounded like a primary school singer. So I was sitting there thinking, "I don't want to do this now." I felt really cack. He'd be all nicey-nicey afterwards – I can't be bothered with people being two-faced like that.'

Nor did she particularly enjoy being filmed all day long. As far as she was concerned, this was her idea of hell: 'You feel really insecure about yourself, but I still had a great time in there. What did it teach me? Never to do karaoke again! It was mad though, and I get recognised a lot more now because of it.'

Although the show's psychologist, Dr Cynthia McVey, agreed with Fearne, she showed a greater interest in some of the other names on the academy roll call when asked to evaluate everyone's hopes. Certainly, she admitted, 'It is a very intriguing mix of people. I don't know if any of them can actually sing or dance, but that's not really the point.

'The choice of women is interesting because Ruby Wax and Jo Brand are very strong, forceful personalities. Contrast them with Ulrika, who is very feminine, very girly and very popular with the men. I would imagine that Ulrika may feel threatened by those two and, if so, she would ally herself to the men. That would make great television and, as it's all for charity, no one's reputation will suffer.'

Interestingly enough, McVey regarded the celebrity participants as being just like the non-celebs who audition for reality TV shows. Each one has a particular reason for agreeing to become exposed to ridicule as the cameras roll, with the main reason, of course, being to raise their profile. In addition, they may want to prove they have other talents we don't already know about, or perhaps it's simply that they want to help the charity.

'Ulrika certainly doesn't need to raise her profile,' McVey continued. 'But she may feel she has something to prove and will want to show the world there is more to her than simply someone who goes out with famous men. I don't know if she's a great singer or dancer, but she'll probably feel that dancing next to Jo Brand she'll look great.'

As for Will, Kwame and Fearne, McVey considered all

three unknown quantities and reckoned viewers would be more impressed by those who had already made a name for themselves. Clearly, she wasn't a regular viewer of Saturday morning television if she didn't recognise Fearne. Even so, before a single note had been sung her personal favourite was Ruby Wax.

'I've met Ruby and she's very smart and not afraid to say what she thinks. She'll be great value for money. Like Jo Brand, I think Ruby will be doing this for fun. She's not worried about making a fool of herself. I don't know much about Paul Ross, but if he's anything like his brother Jonathan, he will be game for anything.

'Much the same as John Thomson from *Cold Feet* [Pete Gifford], who, like Ulrika, doesn't need to raise his public profile, not after the few months he has just gone through, of revelations about his private life [following drink-driving offences]. But the public think they know him from the show and this will be his chance to show us a little of the real John.'

Whether or not McVey had heard of Fearne, it didn't really matter. Soon after her appearance on *Fame Academy* she was named the most popular children's presenter on television. Just like *Blue Peter*'s Valerie Singleton forty years earlier, she had become a role model for thousands of schoolchildren. The difference is that she was also seen as a cool poster girl for teenage boys and men: 'So I present *Top of the Pops* and I've done the occasional stint on *Never Mind the Buzzcocks* but I'm a children's television presenter. That is why I am on television and what I am paid for; that is what I take most seriously. And I get to interview some amazing celebrities and I do go out to loads of gigs in the evening.'

One of those 'amazing celebrities' as far as Fearne was concerned was Pop Princess Kylie Minogue: 'I've met Kylie lots of times and I both love and detest interviewing her. She's the most lovely lady but I feel like a big farmer's wife next to her. She's this petite, gorgeous creature, like a sculpture. I was so sad to hear about her breast cancer, it was a real shock. But if it raises awareness and gets young women to start checking their breasts regularly, at least some good can come of it all.'

Kylie, of course, had burst on to the UK music scene in 1988, just seven years after Fearne was born. Having scored the biggest-selling single ever in Australia that previous year with 'Locomotion', over the next five years she became one of the most successful female recording artists of all time, out-selling and out-surviving almost every one of her contemporaries in much the same way as today. Indeed Kylie is the kind of comeback queen who never went away. Through her own desire to progress, improve and reinvent herself, she has become irreplaceable. She remains untainted and as fresh as the day she first stepped into the spotlight, but with more drive and ambition than ever before.

To date she has released ten studio albums, six long-play videos, greatest hits and live packages, a multitude of other hits and remix compilations and well over forty singles throughout the world, many of which are regarded as pop classics. One of her most successful singles was 'Can't Get You Out of My Head', which ended up being the Number One record in almost every territory in which it was released. Not only that but it has sold literally in its millions, and repeated the same success across America in 2002. And the album *Fever*, from which the single was taken, has enjoyed similar acclaim in Britain and throughout the world. Add to this her successful roles on both the television and movie screen and you have a real rollercoaster ride of a career. Today Kylie could not be more successful if she tried.

Despite launching her own lingerie range, show-casing her ninth album with a 'money can't buy' gig in London and her 'Showgirl' tour being a sell-out, the unexpected happened when she was diagnosed with breast cancer just days before her tour was to open in Australia. She was forced to postpone and take time away from the limelight. With support from her then boyfriend, Hollywood heart-throb Olivier Martinez, with whom she is still the best of friends, and sister Dannii, she wrote a children's book, launched her own

'Darling' perfume and eventually made an emotional return to the stage to resume her tour. After attending the opening of her own exhibition at London's Victoria & Albert Museum, having her global summer beachwear featured by Hennes and joining David Tennant for the Christmas edition of *Doctor Who*, she celebrated her twentieth anniversary as a recording artist in 2007 with the release of her tenth album.

Once again it seemed that her talent had won through despite a major setback that might have ruined a lesser talent and would certainly have crippled a less resolute one. With her determination, Kylie once again shone through, and not for the first time she gained the credit and critical acclaim that had evaded her for so long at the start of her career. Perhaps it's no wonder Fearne both loved and detested interviewing her!

Even if Kylie wasn't at the top of her list of ideal interviewees, Hollywood funny man Jim Carrey was certainly among Fearne's favourites: 'He turned out to be one of the funniest, nicest people I've ever met. He's really sweet and down-to-earth. Robbie Williams is always great, too. He's really honest and you always get something off-the-cuff and random.' And she continues, 'When Marilyn Manson came on, I really loved him and I'm just intrigued by his whole lifestyle and everything; I find him fascinating. I didn't get to meet him but he walked past me in the corridor. I was just plodding along, going to my dressing room, and I just went [gasps], I just froze and he walked past me, and I started following him down the corridor! He had all of his make-up on, and everything. I couldn't believe that Marilyn Manson had just walked past me, it was crazy!'

But without any hesitation, the worst, she says, was Liam Gallagher: 'He was a nightmare! He'd just swear or give one-word answers. I was just thinking, "Liam, you are ruining my dreams!" I presented the Best DVD Award to his brother Noel at the NME Awards and he was as bad. He just came on stage, took the award and didn't even look at me.' Avril Lavigne was another bad interviewee as far as Fearne was concerned: 'She is always a challenge. I don't dislike her – she's probably just difficult because she always has her hair over her eyes. I found her a bit odd.'

If there was anyone she would like to have interviewed at that time, it was Gwen Stefani: 'She's been on the show but I've never actually got to talk to her. I've tried waving, but she didn't really see, so that was quite embarrassing. I was going "Wooo!" and waving and she was just, like, "Nutter", looking away. So yeah, Gwen would be awesome. Who else right now? Oh, also Slash from Guns N' Roses and Velvet Revolver. I'd love to sit down, have a drink and interview him for hours – that would be brilliant!'

Less nerve-racking than interviewing Gallagher and Lavigne was going out to all the gigs she was then attending – about thirty in two months, she reckoned – to see bands such as the Ordinary Boys, Green Day, the Bravery, the Kaiser Chiefs, Velvet Revolver, the Used and the Killers. But she insisted she would never dream of getting completely drunk or behaving in any way that wasn't suitable for the occasion. Listening to her talking, you might be forgiven for thinking her a little pious. After all, we live in a society that seems to laud the more outrageous antics of celebrities. Fearne shakes her head at the suggestion.

It was about six months after *Fame Academy* that the gossip columnists first became interested in her. And perhaps no wonder for this was when she secretly began to date contestant Peter Brame, and as far as the tabloids were concerned, this was headline news.

Although she focused on the gentler side of his personality, the ubiquitous tabloid press and paparazzi found Brame's past and presumably future indiscretions of considerably greater interest than anything she had already seen in him. Even though he had obtained a degree in history and was working as a management trainee when he successfully auditioned for the second series of *Fame Academy*, he quickly became a favourite with the viewing public when he reached the penultimate showdown. Eventually he had finished in fourth place and was praised for his performances and songwriting, but unfortunately this didn't last.

Brame became far more celebrated for his wild behaviour and was branded a 'love rat' by the *Sun* for smooching with ex-lap dancer Carolynne Good on *Fame Academy,* devastating his loyal girlfriend Emma Cook, and for his constant rows with that year's *Academy* winner Alex Parks, rather than anything he achieved after the show ended.

The Academy, of course, had not prepared its students for dealing with the consequences of fame and Brame appeared to struggle with all the attention. His excessive drinking and partying lifestyle made him a perfect target for journalists and the paparazzi; he was written about and photographed so many times looking drunk and dishevelled at parties and clubs that it was obvious he could not cope with his rise to mediocre fame. Before long he had become dependent on recreational drugs as well as alcohol.

He met Fearne when he and fellow *Fame Academy* hopefuls were given leave from their television house to visit the *Top of the Pops'* studio to see the Friday night show being filmed. Fearne interviewed all the *Academy* students on the studio visit but it was she and Peter who got on well and exchanged numbers. They went out a few times and more or less hit it off straight away. If it's true that she goes for the rough-and-ready type, it wasn't surprising that she and Peter ended up as an item because, according to most, 'rough and ready' are the two words that sum him up best.

Making matters worse, just three weeks into his relationship with Fearne, was Peter's confession that he smoked killer crack and took cocaine on a wild night out with a group of topless glamour models after a football match. 'I bitterly regret it,' he admitted at the time. 'I'm no saint and I have dabbled in drugs before. But this was the first time I had taken crack. I've let down the kids who voted for me on *Fame Academy* and want to apologise.' But his revelations caused much more damage than he could possibly fathom – and potentially the greatest harm of all was what this might have done to Fearne's career: his actions could so easily have wrecked her image as the perfect squeaky-clean children's presenter.

It all came at the beginning of the relationship, and according to Fearne, they didn't talk about it much: 'We swept it under the carpet.' The trouble was, 'I've never had anything to do with drugs and it was never anything to do with me, but he wasn't proud of it and was embarrassed that I was caught up in it.' One of the more unfortunate moments for her publicly was when she was pictured leaving a nightclub with Brame, looking like a bleary-eyed rock chick. Even worse was the fact that her BBC bosses were not at all impressed or amused; if anything they were concerned and they feared their golden girl might be heading in the same direction as other disgraced children's presenters such as John Leslie, Richard Bacon and Jamie Theakston. Later, she admitted, 'People at work were quizzing me about the relationship, asking whether it was good for my image. They were slightly concerned and even though they didn't need to, they reminded me it is my responsibility to act in a certain way.'

And of course, they were right: 'Those awful pictures of Peter and I leaving that club did me no favours. It looked like we were paralytic and I was all sweaty and hot. Peter had had a few drinks and was a bit the worse for wear but I just had the worst flu ever. I was really run-down and had taken about five of those fizzy vitamin C tablets to keep going. I came out looking ill and the photographers leapt to the wrong conclusions.'

Anyone who knows Fearne will tell you that she is an incredibly driven, dedicated and disciplined person in everything she does. While concern was raised when friends and employers realised she was indeed going out with Brame, somehow they managed to overlook just how sensible she was and the fact that she would not let the situation get out of control. Then, as much as today, she was very much her own person.

But perhaps, deep inside, she also shared the same concerns. Maybe it was coincidental but isn't it strange that after listening to what they were saying, she did her own bit of soul-searching and, in the end, she decided to cut Brame out of her life for good. They grew apart, but the bad publicity surrounding their romance hadn't helped. Neither had Brame's erratic behaviour. Certainly, when they were out together, he would often become edgy and possessive if she ever chatted to other men. And he would also square up to photographers and bouncers, earning himself a reputation as a third-rate Liam Gallagher.

Even though there were stories of break-ups, reconciliations, engagement rings, not to mention the couple publicly illustrating how together they were by kissing passionately in front of embarrassed bystanders outside such venues as London's Sketch Club at 3am, in the end Peter's hedonistic lifestyle constantly clashed with Fearne's single-minded approach to her career. After nine months, things finally came to a head. 'Peter was a real rock'n'roll party boy, but he took it to another level,' Fearne was to elaborate later. 'He loved going out and hanging out with friends, which made it difficult for us to get along. I'd be getting up really early to go to work and he'd just be coming in after a night on the town. We never got to see each other. It all got a bit intense and we thought it would be better to call it quits.'

Even though she was no veteran of relationships at

that time, and despite the fact that she may have admitted she hadn't really entertained the idea of a serious boyfriend at that point, it did seem as if she was very much in love with Brame. Although the relationship started out as little more than a crush, she did appear to dive in pretty quickly, and perhaps in the process she underestimated the strength of her own emotions. Two months after they met, the couple were living together and a few months after that they were apparently engaged. Not that Fearne had any great plans for marriage.

Neither did it help to be hounded by the tabloid press. Fearne agrees: 'I find it very difficult and very confusing. I do like to go out and I do think it's important to have a profile in the press, but I hate the way you get misrepresented and labelled as one thing. It was really difficult; it was a very bad time for me. I was also portrayed in the same way and that was completely wrong. It was my first serious relationship and everything was carried out in the spotlight. It was a mistake but I hope I learnt a lesson from it – I'm a lot more careful now.'

Neither had she expected Brame to sell a kiss-and-tell story to the *News of the World* in which he revealed how the sex life that she apparently craved, described in eye-watering detail, was scuppered by his destructive cocaine habit. Although he also said some nice things about her in the piece, this was still a scary moment for Fearne: 'I'd never been exposed to the press in that way before and it was weird, especially when my parents read it. It was quite upsetting and difficult to deal with, to be honest, especially when you've lived with someone for eight months and thought you could trust them. He had to do it for his own reasons and I don't resent him for that. But I'm totally over it and it's all been a learning curve. You can't really help who you fall in love with, but you can forgive and forget and move on.'

Chapter 5

Good Times, Bad Times

'I think I have the most fantastic job in the world and every day I am grateful for it. I would like to move into adult television but I accept it won't happen overnight.'

There are times in everyone's life when, suddenly and inexplicably, everything seems to go wrong. Two months after Fearne's twenty-third birthday, Christopher Parker (the friend who played Spencer Moon in *EastEnders*) was closer to that state than he had ever felt before and he attempted to end his life by slashing his wrists and taking an overdose of paracetamol after checking into a London hotel.

He said he was in a desperate state of mind after a woman claimed that he had lied about a relationship to hide the fact that he was gay. He said the gay rumours were false and made him out to be a liar: 'I really wanted it to work. It was never a cry for help – I'd just had enough.'

When *OK!* magazine caught up with him two months later for a January 2005 interview, he admitted that he had taken the tablets and a set of knives with him to the hotel and attempted several times to slash his wrists: 'I was in a lot of pain and I just wanted to pass out. I was in a cycle of sleeping for twenty minutes, puking for twenty minutes and then cutting my wrists for twenty minutes. I tried to jump out of the window but was too scared and kept chickening out.'

Eventually he was discovered by two of his friends, who found him struggling to breathe after losing four pints of blood. He was taken to hospital, where he received stitches and was told that he had done no lasting damage to his body. Although he later reflected that his suicide attempt was foolish, he had reached the stage of desperation when he heard the kiss-and-tell was about to be published: 'I'd had such a successful year and I felt as though it was all about to go down the drain. I didn't want to have to face anyone the next day or have to pick up the pieces; I just wanted an easy way out. It's a coward's way out but I just wanted out.' He had been scheduled to leave *EastEnders* later that same year but following his stay in hospital, he asked the producers to let him go straight away, which they did.

Without specifying whether she was one of the two friends who found Chris struggling to breathe on the floor of the London hotel room, Fearne's eyes still soften whenever she relays his desperation at that time in his life: 'He had the worst time. It's awful to see someone you love go through what he went through. All I could do was be there for him and tell him how much I loved him. I don't think people understand how hard it is to have people say all these things about you and you feel you can't fight back.' Today, he is still one of her best mates: 'I used to interview him a lot and we got really pally. People thought we were an item at first, which is hilarious. He's like my little brother; there's never been anything between us.'

In one late night conversation they both decided not to constantly moan about the bad situations they'd been in, but to focus on how lucky they were. And that's when the idea was formed: 'Chris and I wanted to do something, so we agreed together to go to a country where people had nothing. We wanted to go to schools in Africa and see what kids over there had to put up with. We wanted to present something from our perspective for the people we normally relate to.'

They took their idea to the founder of Red Nose Day, film director Richard Curtis, who signed them up for Comic Relief. Fearne was completely bowled over by him: 'I've met many amazing people, but one man who made me absolutely speechless with admiration and wonder was Richard Curtis. He had absolutely no preconceptions about who we were. He took our idea and was so enthusiastic about it; he helped us by contacting all these people who could make it happen.'

It also helped that Fearne was a huge fan of Curtis's 1994 hit *Four Weddings and a Funeral*, the film that turned Hugh Grant into a star. She remembers, as a child: 'I watched it twice a week. So, when I first met Richard doing *Celebrity Fame Academy*, I was in awe of this man who had written such a genius script. It was only then that I found out about his amazing commitment to Comic Relief and all the charitable aspects of his life.'

Although Richard Curtis was born in New Zealand in 1956 and raised in Manila, Stockholm, Folkestone and Warrington, he has now lived in London, off and on, for over twenty years. He began writing comedy after leaving Oxford University in 1978 and won his first job in television writing sketches for BBC's *Not the Nine O'Clock News*, which in turn led him to write the scripts for Rowan Atkinson's *Blackadder* series, a situation comedy set in four different eras of British history. Although the show won countless awards, it was while he was writing the last three series (with Ben Elton) that he was inspired to stage two West End comedy revues with Atkinson and Elton, which in turn provided him with the idea to script his first film, *The Tall Guy*, directed by Mel Smith and starring Jeff Goldblum, Emma Thompson (in her film debut) and Atkinson as a cruel, heartless comedian starring in a West End show. Even though the film was as successful as he had hoped, he still continued to write for the small screen and once again collaborated with Atkinson on *Mr Bean* in 1990.

By 1993, Curtis had written *Bernard and the Genie*, a wholesome Christmas fantasy starring Lenny Henry and Alan Cumming, and towards the end of that year, he won a Writers Guild of Great Britain Comedy Lifetime Achievement Award. His second film, and probably what he is still best known for, was Fearne's favourite. Released in March 1994, the movie won a French César Award, an Australian Academy Award and the BAFTA for Best Film. At the Academy Awards, it was also up for two nominations: Best Original Screenplay and Best Film.

In the same year as *Four Weddings and a Funeral* hit the screens, Curtis received an MBE in the New Year Honours List while he was working on the script for *The Vicar of Dibley*, a situation comedy for the BBC, starring Dawn French as a female vicar in a small village suspiciously full of eccentric characters. The movie *Bean* – co-written with Robin Driscoll, directed by Mel Smith and starring Atkinson – opened in Britain at the end of August three years after *Four Weddings*. Curtis followed *Bean* with *Notting Hill*, starring Julia Roberts and Hugh Grant, a work that became the highest-earning British film in history and would eventually gross over $350 million. The success of *Notting Hill*, and Curtis's award-winning screenplay *Bridget Jones's Diary*, and his most recent projects *Love Actually*, *Bridget Jones: The Edge of Reason* and *Mr Bean's Holiday* have all helped to establish him among the upper echelons of British screenwriters.

As Fearne had already discovered, Curtis was also responsible for co-producing the live nights of *Comic Relief* for the BBC since 1987, during which time the charity has collected over £325,000,000 for projects both in Africa and in the UK. 'He's just a fantastic individual,' says Fearne. 'He took a whole year out from writing to dedicate himself to *Live 8* and the G8 summit – I don't know how he does it. He's making a huge difference to the planet but also manages to be the most hilarious man on earth at the same time. We'd both worked on *Sports Relief* [for which Fearne joined Nigel Harman, Andrew Marr, Sarah Manners and Nick Knowles to represent the BBC team for a special star-studded episode of *Superstars: Battle of the Channels*] so I'd seen him there. Afterwards, I was chatting to people who'd just got back from filming in Ethiopia and myself and Chris thought, "This is a fantastic way to get involved with Comic Relief, maybe we could go on a trip somewhere?"

'I think that Comic Relief needs to keep the audience as broad as possible: we need to educate children about what's going on out there. And that's quite difficult unless you've actually been there yourself. Because I'd met Richard before, I emailed him and said I would love to be involved, to help put the message across to the younger generation.'

And so, she continues, 'He arranged for Chris and me to visit Kenya for a week – it was just a fantastic trip. We saw some unbelievably awful things out there, but also some brilliant things too. I'm forever grateful that Richard allowed me the opportunity. You'd go to a meeting with him about some pretty serious issues in Africa, but he's always got this most incredible way of communicating things. There are some tragic things happening in the world, but to also show the light-hearted side, that's what Richard does best.'

When she returned from the trip with Chris, she was just as enthusiastic as before: 'I learnt more there than almost anywhere else. We went to the worst slums and visited schools where providing a child with a chair, a pencil and a piece of paper was a major achievement. We are so unaware of how lucky we are. When Chris and I came back, we were both blown away by the fact the toilets flushed. This is something that we take for granted yet there are people who have to walk miles for clean water; it makes me want to cry. I really hope our film can do something to add to the amazing things Comic Relief achieves.

'We visited lots of slums and orphanages. We went to this slum that had 20,000 people living in it and not one toilet in the whole place. There was no food or water, 40 per cent of the people had AIDS and cholera was rife as a result of terrible sanitation. More positively, we saw a building project. If a person can raise a small sum of money towards a house, then Comic Relief will pay for the rest and teach them the skills to build their own house. Once they've learnt how, they can build extra rooms on to the house and rent them out to help get other people out of the slums, so it becomes a positive cycle of helping people. We also visited feeding stations that enable children to go and get food for themselves and their families – those who haven't been wiped out by AIDS – so they can eat without having to leave school and work.'

During an interview with BBC Radio Berkshire, Fearne reinforced how great the experience had been and couldn't help but recount her visit to Kibera, a huge slum just outside Nairobi: 'We drove up and there was a blanket of corrugated iron ... people walking around in this road area ... people selling fruit, meat with flies buzzing around it ... meant to keep their stalls a hundred metres away from the train tracks and people are only a metre from it. We walked over a bridge, over a stream that was not a stream ... it was basically absolutely full of rubbish, old food, even a dead dog, face down in all this muck. And this water doubles up with what they cook with – they have no proper water supplies, no sanitation, no toilets anywhere. It's crazy!'

At the time of Fearne's visit with Chris, East Africa had over 12 million city dwellers living in slums and that number is still growing to this day despite the efforts of the authorities who will often try to remove inhabitants by force. The Nyando district of Western Kenya is one of the worst affected by HIV and AIDS. There are few medical centres or schools and a higher rate of illness and death than anywhere else. Around 20,000 of the children are orphans and they are indeed a frightening legacy of such terrible – and unbelievable – conditions.

It is refreshing to think that many of those children seek out a better life in the city. And that was why Fearne wanted to meet the street kids to find out how this vulnerable community gets by: 'We had 50 kids following us down the road, like the Pied Piper. We were filming, taking photos … And then I noticed they were all carrying these little bottles with milk or something in the bottom. Then Joshua was saying that they all have little pots of glue and they sniff it because it gets them high and helps them forget if it gets cold at night. And that's just how they live every day.'

Alarming as that is, it's estimated there are over 20,000 orphans in some parts of Western Kenya, many of whom will end up on the streets of towns and cities where life can be very harsh. Towards the end of her trip, Fearne made a friend she will never forget: Susan lived in a house with twelve people – her three children, her mother, father plus other relatives. The living conditions were so cramped that she had to sleep outside to ensure there was enough room for everyone else. Susan is also HIV positive and her upbeat attitude to life really left a mark on the young presenter when they hung out together: 'How can you not think about being HIV positive day to day? I really felt like I was friends with Susan – we chatted and we hugged ... She was really happy. She said, "Now we are friends!" And I thought, I didn't really want to leave her.' In Africa, there are few who have not already lost someone they love to AIDS and the trauma of living with this terrible disease puts huge pressure on families.

So moving was Fearne's trip that as soon as she got home, she immediately wanted to do more: 'I came back with a real passion for it because I saw the things the money was helping with. You see stuff on TV and it can be disheartening but to see the positive side too was a really uplifting experience. It's such a worthwhile cause and it's so easy to help: you just buy a red nose and have fun.'

And that is exactly what she did a year later when she and Jonathan Ross teamed up to kick off the first hour of proceedings for the Red Nose Telefon. Red Nose Day, of course, is the highlight of Comic Relief's fund-raising campaign and takes place in March every other year. Not only do the whole of Britain spend the day raising cash any way they could but Comic Relief itself take over the normal schedules on BBC1 with their own programmes that included specially recorded shows, studio guests and live reports throughout the night.

Soon after Red Nose Day, Fearne talked about how she felt she had reached that difficult position where she wanted to make the leap from being a children's presenter to take on a more adult role. She was only too aware that she needed to avoid falling down 'the great big void that lies between the two' and so she started to spread the word that in future she was interested in presenting jobs that weren't just for children. She admitted at the time, 'I think I have the most fantastic job in the world and every day I am grateful for it. I would like to move into adult television but I accept it won't happen overnight. I love people like Jonathan Ross and Davina McCall. Actually, Davina must think I'm a complete idiot because I saw her at a Christmas party and I ran up to her and started going on. When I'm nervous, I talk all the time and I grin like an idiot. I remember the words, "I love you, Davina" coming out of my mouth. Luckily she was very sweet back.'

Fearne's decision to step away from children's shows and into something more adult-like really started when she took on the new-look Sunday evening edition of *Top of the Pops* as the main presenter. The show was extended from 30 to 45 minutes, and, as always, she was very excited and couldn't quite believe that she was now anchorwoman for the programme she had so loved while growing up.

It was, after all, Britain's longest-running and arguably most important pop music show on television, if only because this was the sole regular spot for audiences to see chart acts, especially American ones, prior to the advent of dedicated music channels such as MTV. Despite the increased competition, *Top of the Pops* had simple packaging of the singles chart, which, even to this day in the age of digital downloads, is still remembered as one of its most popular features and while *TOTP* was on air, it challenged longevity and turned a show only intended to last six weeks into a national institution.

The first *Top of the Pops* was presented by DJ Jimmy Savile on New Year's Day in 1964 and featured, among others, Dusty Springfield and the Rolling Stones. Its formula, developed by the show's first producer Johnnie Stewart, proved an immediate success. The only criteria that an artist or band needed to have to appear on the programme was that they had to have a single already climbing the Top 20.

For many years, all the acts mimed or lip-synched to their records, a habit still widespread to this day in music television circles, but in the early days of *Top of the Pops* the fact was made surprisingly explicit. Singles were visibly placed on a turntable in front of the presenter and 'spun' by an assistant. But the novelty of seeing, rather than just hearing performers and the disclosure of 'this week's best-selling single' quickly made *Top of the Pops* essential viewing for young singles-buyers.

The impact of the programme was immediate. According to Fearne's grandfather's cousin, Bill Cotton, then BBC's Assistant Head of Light Entertainment, the Beatles' manager Brian Epstein rang up after the second broadcast and asked if the band's new single could be played on the show. Realising his luck, Cotton insisted the Beatles appear in person, knowing the resulting pandemonium would be the kind of publicity money couldn't buy.

But he wasn't so fortunate in his attempts to get Elvis Presley on the show (one of Fearne's favourites, whose picture she once had on her MySpace). Presley and his manager Colonel Parker declined all television guest appearances and Parker even refused to allow any clips to be shown of Elvis singing his latest hit from his most recent movie, either then or in the future. He wanted to avoid any kind of overexposure that would cut into movie profits or discourage fans from paying the price of a cinema ticket to see Elvis sing on the big screen.

Other acts of the day weren't quite so difficult to get hold of, although naturally there were times when some were unavailable and nine times out of ten when that happened, they at least provided a specially filmed performance to substitute their absence, and when that wasn't available (as with Elvis), those stalwarts, the Go-Jos, Pan's People, Ruby Flipper and Legs and Co would step in with their choreographed routines and skimpy outfits that proved particularly popular with male viewers and studio audiences. Over time, and with the introduction of specially shot videos, plus a reliance on pre-recorded material during the late-1980s, the dancers were seen less and less, and the loss of both elements consequently began to dent the show's popularity. A return to studio performances restored the programme's fortunes, breathing new life into what many considered was becoming an ageing slogan: 'It's number one ... it's *Top of the Pops*!'

In many ways, introducing Fearne was part of the process of breathing new life into the show during the noughties, and this of course provided her with the fantastic opportunity to hang out with, meet and interview some of her own childhood heroes, along with whichever guest presenter was brought in to help her negotiate her way through the hits and live performers.

To start with, it was all very experimental, she remembers, 'because every presenter is so different so I had to adapt to whoever we had on, which kept me on my toes. But I never felt I was holding the show together. I'm a massive fan of Jeremy Clarkson – who presented the first one – and Richard Bacon and I got some great banter going because we're mates anyway.' Either way, she always sang the praises of her guest presenters, no matter who they were, despite the fact that some of them didn't look exactly comfortable with the live format.

One of her happiest memories is when Duran Duran appeared on the show on her birthday: 'Reggie [Yates] and I were dancing like loons at the side of the stage during their performance and Simon was well impressed with us. I gave him my email address and he wrote to me and sent me an album. Simon Le Bon emailed me! Wow, I was so excited to meet him, I was grinning like a Cheshire cat!' She still has a photo taken from that night pinned on her kitchen wall: 'I come downstairs every morning to make a cuppa and say, "Morning, Simon!"'

Another time, she still remembers fondly, was, 'When U2 were on, and myself and Reg were about to introduce them at the beginning of the show. We just turned to each other and went, "How did we get from *Disney Club* to introducing U2 on *Top of the Pops*, how did *that* happen?" It was like a fast-forward from there to that point, and it was really crazy!'

One of her most alarming moments, however, was when her mother bought her a pair of silk knickers with diamanté buttons up the back for her birthday: 'When I promised I'd wear them under a classy dress on *Top of the Pops* that night, she was thrilled. Five minutes before I was due on, I went to the loo, bent over and, piaow, the diamanté went everywhere! I had to do the entire show with no knickers. I spent the whole time praying there were no fans or wind machines nearby.'

Even though she loved what she was doing and continued to describe herself as the 'luckiest blimmin' person alive', she still valued her private moments away from the cameras. 'I really need that quiet time at home to just be myself,' she explained. 'I enjoy being at opposite ends of the spectrum. I can be really "out there" and chatty at work and then I go home to be peaceful. You can't be full on all the time, you'd burn out.'

One of the ways she would relax and wind down was to sit down, turn the lights out and try to think of nothing. Another was to listen to the meditation tapes that her mother introduced her to as a young child: 'I still have them, but on my iPod instead. They take you on a journey in your head. There's one that takes you to the moon, one to the desert and one that takes you through a house that represents your chakras. It's all a bit odd but it works.'

Something else that she valued highly was her

rebirthing experience: 'Yeah, I found it fascinating. I didn't think I would be very into it as I'm quite a guarded person. You get taken back to the womb. I was crying and making weird noises and revealing stuff that I wouldn't normally tell anyone. I found it totally shocking but I let out all these emotions. It was an amazing, hypnotic experience.' The rebirthing ceremony was carried out by one of her mother's friends. It 'was like a trance', Fearne recalls. 'My body tensed up, and I was crying and telling her all this stuff I didn't know was in there. I came to and I didn't know where I was. It helps you to unblock things and sort out your fears. I'd been going through a weird patch because I'd just broken up with Pete and I needed a chance to let it all out.' She did that as well …

Chapter 6

In With a Chance

'I had the best time, interviewing the people I adore and respect so much. It was an incredible feeling being among the crowd. And I was really flattered by Robbie.'

By July 2005 it seemed as if Fearne had the BBC at her feet. The success of *The Saturday Show* and *Smile* firmly established her in the top league of children's television presenters. So it seemed harsh when TV reporter Danielle Lawler of the *Sunday Mirror* decided to be critical of the way in which Fearne was running up some 200,000 air miles at a cost to the TV licence payer of between £25,000 and £35,000 simply to allow her to keep her dream job as the face of *Top of the Pops*.

Although she had found it quite a different experience

to be presenting both *Top of the Pops* main show and *Top of the Pops Saturday*, Fearne still loved doing both because they each had their own special character: 'We have an audience on the Friday night so it's more of a party atmosphere and everyone's having a dance and all that sort of thing. On *Top of the Pops Saturday*, I get to chat to the bands more and get to have a conversation with them and hang out with them. They've both got their different strong points which I love, but it's quite a different vibe because *Top of the Pops Saturday* is kind of like the chill-out day after the big mad party, which is quite cool!'

And of course when she wasn't doing *Top of the Pops* that summer, she was flying 9,000 miles every week between Britain and the US so that she could make a new children's show with one of her best friends and fellow *Smile* presenter, Reggie Yates. But she had only agreed to do it if she could still front *Top of the Pops* and if the BBC would foot her flight bills. For the first six weeks of production on *Only In America*, she had been flying to New York or Boston for around £466 return, but halfway through shooting, she switched to business class and started flying to and from Orlando, Florida, which at that time was estimated to be at a cost of around £2,000 per trip.

Even so, she must have felt like a world-weary traveller with all the trekking back and forth for three months between July and October, when filming was completed. In one weekend, she recalls, 'I flew in from Miami and slept all day when I got home. Then on Sunday I did *Top of the Pops* with Jeremy Clarkson. The following Saturday I was filming in Orlando and then I would fly home on Sunday and try to get some sleep.'

Even if she wasn't struggling with the schedules she was putting herself under, there must have been times when she felt run-down even if she didn't show it. But to her way of thinking this was simply an inconvenience because filming over in America was such a blast. She remembers, 'The show is basically just me and Reggie going round the US in a Mustang. We're great mates so it's such a laugh. We've already stayed on a ranch, seen the shuttle launch and been to a high school prom. Reggie became a jock and I became a cheerleader, it was hilarious. It's our version of *The Simple Life*, except me and Reg aren't quite as glam as Paris and Nicole.'

Indeed, if it was a 'blast', as Fearne describes, then it wasn't that surprising. To many the show must have seemed more like a road trip of a lifetime in which she and Reggie discovered some of the more bizarre and wonderful things that the US had to offer. From Florida to Hollywood and Manhattan to Seattle and Vegas, where they found diners, donuts, shoe trees and someone who thought they were Elvis, filming took almost three months to complete as they witnessed pretty much everything that any tourist to America would want to see, but wouldn't be able to fit into a standard annual vacation. It was the perfect travelogue for children's television.

And 'blast' is exactly how singing cowboy Pioneer Pepper remembers the experience when he got a call from the BBC to ask if he and his Sunset Pioneers' tribute to the memories of singing cowboys would be interested in taking part in the show: 'It all started with a phone call from across the pond in April 2005. Sarah West from the BBC called and wanted to know if we could film for a new TV series coming out in the fall of 2005. She was a delight to talk to and we were able to get the ball rolling pretty quickly with all the details to confirm our spot on the show.

'Once we were confirmed for the western segment of the ten-part series, the real fun started. I had to write our performance segment and look for a site for filming that would fit into the producer and director's vision for the show. It was a neat process to be involved in. With the ideas pretty much down, the next step was to finalise the actual filming sequences to follow the story lines.

'It was now time to meet face to face with the director Paul Giddings and researcher Ruth Mills to iron out all the details. They flew in from the BBC and met me at the Old Tucson Studios, where it was determined we would film our segment of the programme. Paul and Ruth were both absolutely wonderful to work with and we had a great time from the moment we met. We spent the day at the studio, going over locations where to film, and sharpening the story line to our show so everybody had a good idea of how the format was to flow. A week later we were scheduled to shoot.

'The day of the shoot was absolutely brilliant. Now I picked up a few new words in my vocabulary from our allies across the pond. "Brilliant" and "lovely" were two of our favourites and for weeks after the shoot we were still saying them! We started shooting at 7am! This was coming from a show the night before, so I do have to mention that the good ol' cowboy coffee was flowing like a flooded stream after a monsoon storm. The first three hours of filming was done on a closed set and this is when we first met the hosts of the show. Fearne and Reggie were the TV stars and presenters of the series. It was fun to watch them work and they definitely looked great in their cowboy clothes. We outfitted them with cowboy hats, cowboy scarves, and then gave them their instruments that they were going to need to perform with us on the stage segment of the show. Fearne got the washboard and Reg got the spoons.

'Paul the director wanted Cassandra and Calena to be the ones to teach Fearne and Reg how to play "cowboy" style. It was a hoot! They performed brilliantly (there's that word again). Once all the backstage and onstage instructions were filmed, we were ready to open the doors for 3,000 kids that attended Old Tucson Studios and start the show. We filmed for several more hours, doing our performance segment over and over so the camera crews were able to get all the angles and material that the director wanted. The creative process was really an interesting thing to watch; I love the behind-the-scenes kind of stuff. The filming ended in the late afternoon and we were back at the ranch later that evening.

'It was a sixteen-hour day for the Sunset Pioneers but it was so packed full of exciting memories for us. We certainly enjoyed the royal treatment from our new friends across the pond in England.'

On top of everything else, by the time filming for *Only In America* was complete, Fearne had joined Radio 1 every Friday morning for the 4 to 7am shift. But it was the gig she won a couple of months earlier that she and many others regard as the highlight of her career so far when she presented Live 8 in July 2005, in London's Hyde Park, and found herself being chatted up by Robbie Williams. During an interview, he asked her on-camera in front of 29 million viewers to go and live with him and his dogs in Los Angeles. But she preferred to remain just friends.

Jonathan Ross kick-started the BBC's coverage from Hyde Park, with Jo Whiley and Fearne catching the bands as they came on- and off-stage. Viewers were able to see the whole of the gig live, together with the best of the music from similar events in Paris, Berlin, Lisbon and Rome. Bob Geldof, Bono, Sir Paul McCartney, Madonna, Robbie Williams, Elton John, Sting and Chris Martin were just some of the big names to be interviewed.

Special studio guests were Michael Buerk, Jools Holland, George Alagiah, Sanjeev Baskhar and Meera Syal, and in America Graham Norton was on hand to host the live coverage from Philadelphia. Like Fearne, he would be reporting from backstage and bringing viewers all the gossip and news as it happened as well as interviewing artists and groups such as 50 Cent, Bon Jovi, the Kaiser Chiefs, Maroon 5, P. Diddy and Stevie Wonder.

'I had the best time,' Fearne enthused, 'interviewing the people I adore and respect so much. It was an incredible feeling being among the crowd. And I was really flattered by Robbie. He's great and I always look forward to interviewing him when he's in the UK.

'We've got similar personalities and get on really well as mates. I'm always happy to be linked with Robbie, he's a dish. But there's no romance, I'm afraid.'

Robbie Williams, of course, has been the biggest pop phenomenon in Britain since the Beatles – and probably in the world – since Elvis. In public and onstage he is the ultimate showman but despite his celebrity profile he has always remained something of an enigma. From a childhood blighted by the desertion of his father, his unconditional love for his mother, his breakthrough in boy band Take That, followed by a descent into drink and drugs, and his later subsequent rise to stratospheric success as a solo artist have been unequalled.

With a record-breaking 14 Brit Awards, 11 Number One singles, an £80 million record deal with EMI (the label made famous by the Beatles) and tours that sell out in literally hours, Robbie has been at the top and bottom of an often-troubled career with triumphs and disasters on the rocky path to his unrivalled position as the nation's number one entertainer.

If Fearne had any concerns about getting together with him, was it any wonder? Robbie is as famous for the women in his life as he is for his music. And perhaps her prime concern was the well-known fact that loneliness had already led him through a series of seemingly meaningless sexual encounters with Nicole Appleton, and, reportedly, Geri Halliwell, Nicole Kidman, Kylie Minogue and Rachel Hunter. Despite all that, Fearne still thought that he was just being cheeky: 'But that's his personality … But it was blown up out of all proportion in the papers the next day. He's really charismatic, a great guy and a gorgeous bloke, but I don't think it's very realistic having a relationship with him. I think he's sort of looking, maybe, for a wife and I still want at least a good five years of fun as a single girl.'

But then again, it's not difficult to work out why someone like Robbie would fall for the presenter he affectionately calls 'Cutie Cotton' or why the BBC's early morning children's shows have such a strong following from men in their mid-twenties to early-forties: 'By the end of the interview I thought he was absolutely gorgeous. I then heard that he apparently fancied me. I kept hearing it from all these people but never actually from him. I met him again later and I was embarrassed because of everything that had been said since the last interview, but still he said nothing. He was just funny and gorgeous and chatty, but nothing else. It's so annoying because I think he's absolutely amazing and I really fancy him.'

All the same, there was a time before Live 8 when the *Mirror* revealed that Robbie was quite desperate for a date with Fearne. He had, after all, given her a lingering kiss on a *TOTP* appearance and told pals she was gorgeous. But Fearne seems to prefer grungy types. As one *TOTP* insider observed, 'It's no surprise these men are falling over themselves to get to know Fearne. She's great-looking and has a fun personality; she's not just another bland telly babe.'

Not long after the infamous interview, Fearne was thinking about how she would like to put on her own art exhibition of rock stars and as she had already got Robbie to promise that he would sit for her while she painted him, she decided that she would finally do something about it as soon as she found a break in her schedule. She also had some ideas about how to portray some of her other favourite musicians such as Ozzy Osbourne, Marilyn Manson and the Strokes.

But because rock stars' schedules are always at a premium she had already worked out that the best way would perhaps be to paint the artists who weren't available in person from photographs rather than to wait to depict them from real life. She had even thought about a location to hold the exhibition once she had all the portraits complete and ready to show to the public. A venue that was a strong possibility, she thought, would be Camden's Proud Galleries, which had recently displayed photos by Pete Doherty. It still remains something she has to do, although with her time even more at a premium, perhaps it is something that will have to wait for now.

Interestingly enough, it was when Doherty joined Elton John for a version of T-Rex's 'Children of the Revolution' on the Live 8 stage, evidently drunk and worse for wear, and when Fearne saw Kate Moss, his then-girlfriend, watching anxiously backstage, that she was reminded of her own past. There, in front of her, stood the hard-living pop star seemingly hell-bent on destruction; at his side, the understanding girlfriend, blindly hoping to keep it all together. Two years previously she had found herself in much the same situation while dating Peter Brame.

With or without Doherty, Live 8 was still criticised in some quarters, even if it was a great idea. As Steve Jones wrote in his online review: 'Whatever your views of the cause – of Bob Geldof, of the "Make Poverty History" campaign or the calibre of bands taking part – Live 8 was always destined to be unequivocally memorable television. In this sense it was exactly like the Golden Jubilee, the General Election, even like the Eurovision Song Contest: all events with which you may feel absolutely zero affinity or sympathy, but which once married up with the small screen become occasions that demand to be watched. It's all down to the way TV can unleash moments of drama in such a fashion as to catch you off-guard and leave you choked with emotion. You knew Live 8 was, by definition, always going to deliver something along these lines, something that reminded you of how TV is a peerless source of popular entertainment. Just what that something would turn out to be was, naturally, the most exciting aspect of the day.'

'Certainly,' he continues, 'surely only those without any heart would claim they weren't moved in some small way at some point by what they saw on their TV set during the ensuing ten hours? And there were plentiful moments of high emotion and catharsis if you wanted them, some probably working better on television than in Hyde Park. U2's release of several dozen white doves from the stage; Bob Geldof's shameless solo stab at "I Don't Like Mondays"; a tiny Annie Lennox singing "Why?" dwarfed by a sequence of images of young African AIDS victims; Madonna's meticulously choreographed hoofing; Robbie Williams's similarly calculated derring-do; Pink Floyd's stately last waltz – all these felt as if they gained something from being reduced for the small screen and then repackaged for the world at large.'

Even so, the idea behind Live 8 seemed to be a solid one: to put on a string of benefit concerts that took place in the G8 states and in South Africa. They were timed to precede the G8 conference and summit held at the Gleneagles Hotel in Auchterarder, Scotland, from 6 to 8 July 2005 and also coincided with the twentieth anniversary of Live Aid. Run in support of the aims of the UK's 'Make Poverty History' campaign and the Global Call for 'Action Against Poverty', the shows were planned to pressurise world leaders to drop the debt of the world's poorest nations, increase and improve aid, and negotiate fair trade rules in the interests of poorer countries. Ten simultaneous concerts were held on 2 July and one on 6 July. On 7 July the G8 leaders pledged to double 2004 levels of aid to poor nations from $25 billion to $50 billion by the year 2010. And half of that money was pledged to go to Africa, a cause very close to Fearne's own heart.

On top of that, more than 1,000 musicians performed at the concerts, which were broadcast on 182 television networks and 2,000 radio networks. Live Aid and Band Aid organiser Bob Geldof announced the event on 31 May with many former Live Aid acts offering their services. Prior to the official announcement, many news sources referred to the event as Live Aid 2. However, Geldof and co-organiser Midge Ure of Ultravox fame have since stated explicitly that they don't consider the event to be the same as Live Aid. Geldof said: 'This is not Live Aid 2. These concerts are the start point for the Long Walk to Justice, the one way we can all make our voices heard in unison.'

Although there were some critics who thought the millionaire rock stars could make a greater contribution by donating parts of their personal fortunes, most of the performers involved had been out of the public eye, which of course encouraged other criticisms that the concerts were being used so that they could get back 'into the spotlight'. Some even argued that Live 8 wasn't intended to raise money but to raise awareness and apply political pressure. And that was probably true.

One month before she was being proposed to by Robbie Williams, and for almost a year before that, Fearne had been dating Lostprophets frontman Ian

Watkins. They had gone public with their relationship at the *Kerrang!* Awards in August 2004, just two weeks after they met at a live outside broadcast of *Top of the Pops* in Newcastle. That was when they were spotted canoodling in the corner and enjoying a very passionate kiss before later leaving to catch a cab outside the venue together.

When she first set eyes on him in Newcastle, she thought, 'My God, he's so fit! A group of us went out for a drink that night but he went to bed early because he was tired. But we started emailing each other, then we started dating. It's nothing too heavy, which suits us both.'

On top of that, she recalls, the Newcastle gig was 'just the best show ever. There was such a great atmosphere, everyone there was having fun, the sun was shining, everyone was up staying the night, and we had some brilliant bands on. It was just the best, best show and we talk about it all the time still.'

Like Tom Jones, Lostprophets hail from Pontypridd in Wales. They had been around for almost a decade when Fearne met Watkins, although the band's musical focus had shifted dramatically in that time from experimental ska and rap to hardcore alternative heavy metal and rock, characterised by the recordings they were making at the time of the *Kerrang!* Awards.

Although Fearne was not screaming her emotions out

loud, it was obviously apparent that she felt much more comfortable about her relationship with Watkins than she ever did with Peter Brame. It also helped that this time the tabloids weren't always on her back or concocting absurdities. Like so many other celebrities, she knew only too well how pernicious the influence of the tabloid press could be.

What probably pleased them both, though, was that they rarely made headline news or the showbiz gossip columns and were for the most part left alone. Nor did they live in the heady rock'n'roll world of wild partying, preferring a much quieter lifestyle. 'Ian is straight-edged. He doesn't drink, doesn't smoke, doesn't do drugs,' Fearne explained. 'He's really into clean-living, which is what I wanted in my life.'

Even though there were rumours doing the rounds at the time when she met Watkins that she was about to start dating Christopher Parker, nothing could be further from the truth. Fearne had never suggested she was anything more than just friends with Parker. Besides, according to her friends, Watkins was much more her type. He had that rock star rebel image that she loved so much in a guy and much the same philosophy: 'I'd date anyone if they're cool. They've got to be attractive, visually, and then personality kicks in – and if that's not there, you knock it on the head.'

Even when they broke up (in June 2005), there wasn't

much fuss made about the couple going their separate ways, although it was always questionable whether the songs 'Always All Ways' and '4:AM Forever' that Watkins had penned for the band's third album, *Liberation Transmission*, were about their break-up. To this day he refuses to confirm either way; Fearne isn't sure either. Nor is she convinced about another song he wrote called 'Broken Hearts, Torn Up Letters and the Story of a Lonely Girl' that she lists on her all-time favourite soundtracks to her life: 'I don't know if it was written about me but it's a great break-up song. Any split is hard as you're used to being with a person and suddenly they're not in your life. I think the best thing to do is to go out with your girly mates and do all the things you couldn't do in a relationship.' And that is exactly what she did.

Chapter 7

Fiji Blues

'I've never been on such an exposing show in a primetime slot every night. To step out from under that security blanket of my usual music shows is really exciting but obviously nerve-racking too.'

Ten months after Live 8, Fearne jumped the BBC ship and defected to Fiji to host *Love Island* for ITV, joining her former *Comic Relief* comrade Patrick Kielty to front the second series of the six-week tropical reality show. 'I was hooked on the last series, so I am really excited that I'm going to be packing up my flip-flops and setting off to the sun. This time round, I won't just be gossiping about the show with my mates but the whole country!' she enthused.

The programme also offered her the ideal opportunity

to do what she loves doing best – matchmaking. 'There's not enough romance in this world, so I hope the blokes on the island are romantic and woo the ladies. You've got to be yourself because the public will quickly see through an act,' she explained. 'If you've got bad habits, show them, warts and all!'

It seemed she had got the gig because the ITV bosses had struggled to find someone willing to replace the previous year's presenter, model-actress Kelly Brook, who was criticised for being wooden and having a lack of chemistry with Kielty. Even though Denise Van Outen, Lisa Tarbuck and Daisy Donovan were screen-tested to present the series, they all turned it down. But, as Paul Jackson, ITV director of entertainment and comedy, said at the time, 'Fearne is perfect for the show.'

And it couldn't have come at a better time for her. Just weeks before she headed out to Fiji, she had broken up with her then boyfriend, Luke Pritchard, frontman for indie band the Kooks. They had been dating ever since they met three months earlier, but Fearne had apparently grown tired of his lack of attention and so she ended their romance.

The relationship came to an abrupt halt following a big night at the Ibiza Rocks launch at London's Sin Club. It was there that one of those ubiquitous 'friends' revealed that despite Luke being just Fearne's type, and although he had been very keen at the start, he had become overwhelmed with the Kooks' recent successes and unfortunately developed a cocky attitude because of it. He was receiving lots of fan mail and offers from groupies and that's when all the attention seems to have gone to his head. According to the 'friend': 'The first bust-up was early in May after which he begged for another chance. They saw each other at the Ibiza Rocks launch but it was pretty apparent that it wasn't going to work. By the end of the night there was a lot of tension and it was obvious strong words were exchanged. Fearne said, then and there, she didn't want to see him again and he was gutted. Now Luke thinks that he played it too cool and lost out.'

And of course, for several weeks after they went their separate ways, there were the usual rumours about why the couple had broken up. Some even suggested Fearne may have 'dumped' him because of the question raised in the band's hit 'Eddie's Gun', which was written about Luke's experiences of premature ejaculation. She had nothing to say on that particular subject, however, and thought it best simply to let that kind of speculation drift over her head. Without specifying their reasons, the *Mirror*, though, was surprised the relationship lasted as long as it did.

What was strange was that just six weeks after getting together, Luke (who interestingly enough had also dated secondary school sweetheart Lily Allen and then Katie Melua) was getting on so well with Fearne that everything was going along as perfectly as it could, but there were rising tensions during a *Top of the Pops*' taping.

It happened when flustered bosses tried to replace the audience with BBC staff after a legal blunder prevented them using members of the public and Fearne was doing her best to avoid Katie, who was performing her then new single 'Spider's Web'. It was the first time the two women had been in the same room together. As one observer noted, 'There was definite tension between them but Fearne looked the most nervous. She was glad when it was all over.' Not that it appeared to bother Katie or her spokesman: 'She and Luke split up last summer but are still friends. I doubt she would have been creating a scene!'

Fearne and Luke made their first public outing at an intimate XFM Kooks gig at north London's Islington Academy. Despite the fact that it was early days, they seemed quite smitten, even though a spokesman for the Kooks would only say that they were just good friends.

But if she had felt anything about the breakdown of her relationship with Luke, she didn't let this show: she simply consoled herself in private while the tabloid press was quick to suggest that she may have fallen into dating Patrick Kielty, and this led to speculation whether love may have already been in blossom on the celebrity love island long before the cameras started to roll.

According to some sources, they were spotted enjoying a wild night out together at London's exclusive Boujis club, where it seemed Kielty was pulling out all the stops to impress her. From what observers noted, it seemed as if he was definitely on a love island of his own when the couple were dirty dancing together.

As one reporter remarked, 'He looked like he was in heaven. He couldn't get enough of her and didn't leave her side all night. Not many punters recognised her at first as she's a bit of a rock chick and doesn't usually hang out at trendy places like Boujis, a favourite haunt of Princes William and Harry. But she looked stunning and was all glammed up in black. She was loving all the attention Kielty was showering on her. There seemed to be a real spark there, especially when they started dancing.' And again, he made no secret of his attraction to her. It was only a few months before the start of *Love Island* that he admitted in the *Mirror* to having feelings for her when he described her as 'ballsy, spunky and attractive'.

Fearne may well have had the same feelings. 'Well, I would like a boyfriend,' she admitted, when drawn on the subject. 'And Paddy is the funniest man alive and a lovely guy too.' And of course the press were only too keen to let everyone know that Kielty had previously been dating model and presenter Amanda Bryam for four years and had also been romantically linked to Cat Deeley, although both insisted they were nothing more than just good friends.

The first series of *Celebrity Love Island* appeared on our screens in the same month that the sixth series of Channel 4's *Big Brother* kicked off, but unlike *Big Brother*, *Love Island* attracted all kinds of controversy from the moment it was announced by ITV. And one of the biggest objections was the criticism over the format of the show. To many, it seemed this was yet another reality show put out there to attract the highest possible audience.

Following the launch, the celebrities were criticised by viewers for being boring and even the celebrity status of some of the participants was questioned. There was some suspicion as to whether the contestants were simply using the programme as a free holiday, for which, the tabloids claimed, producers held crisis meetings to figure out how to keep things interesting. And soon after that, another tirade began when the tabloid press claimed that the show's original presenters, Kelly Brook and Patrick Kielty, were engaged in a bitter feud. Problems between them had allegedly started after Kielty told viewers on the live show that Brook had previously been involved in a relationship with one of the contestants, Paul Danan from *Hollyoaks*, who ended up being the real star of the show. He made a move on three of the women in turn and was almost kicked out after a drunken row with the eventual winner, nightclub owner Fran Cosgrave.

But even Danan's antics were not enough to keep viewers interested. One of the producers' biggest concerns was how an early episode failed to muster up two million viewers. In an attempt to spice up the whole thing, the producers recruited American *Playboy* centrefold, model and actress Nikki Ziering, to see if she could help liven things up. It seemed she could ... Not long after arriving on the island, she threw herself into a fling with Paul Danan and although their relationship made headline news after the couple shared a bed together, they never offered an answer to the rumours and speculation about having sex, on- or off-camera.

There were other reasons, though, why things weren't working out as they should. Tantamount was Kelly Brook. In preproduction, she demanded that she should be taken on as consultant producer on the programme but with the mounting problems, one cannot help wondering if, in hindsight, she regretted that decision. Her newly found status meant she had to endure a three-hour crisis meeting with TV bosses in a bid to save the £15 million flop from sinking altogether without trace. The ailing show's senior staff gathered for panic talks on Fiji's Bounty Island in a desperate bid to come up with ways to save the programme from further disaster. After a gruelling think-tank, Kelly arrived back on the mainland looking more miserable than ever.

As one insider whispered, 'Everyone on the crew knows the celebrities just aren't performing – they're not doing enough. The idea of putting two young celebs together in the Love Shack turned into the most boring television ever seen because Lady Isabella Hervey lay on her back all day – she looked like a bronzed corpse!

'The producers called their whole team together to hammer out ways of breathing new life into the show and forcing the celebrities to do more entertaining things. At the moment, it just looks like all these people are treating the show as a free holiday.'

At the same time rumours were rife that ITV was about to pull the series if things didn't get any better within two weeks. As one source confirmed, 'Everyone is worried it will go the same way as *Celebrity Wrestling* if it doesn't improve.' (After just five weeks, *Celebrity Wrestling* was moved from its primetime Saturday evening slot to Sunday mornings due to extremely poor ratings and being comprehensively beaten in audience share by BBC1's *Doctor Who*. It was received with derision by professional wrestling fans due to the lack of actual wrestling content.)

And it wasn't just that the problems on the programme were simply with the so-called celebrities: it turned out that presenters Kielty and Brook were proving a handful as well. Brook developed a stern and bizarre refusal to wear a bikini and Kielty started to take full advantage of an agreement to give him picture approval. During one weekend, the pair took part in a lengthy photoshoot with the aim of providing a variety of shots for publicity use but only one ended up on the show's official website.

As one reporter from the *Mirror* discovered, 'The presenters were given authorisation and nothing could be released without their agreement. Patrick insisted there was only one that he liked and vetoed all the others.' Chiefs were further devastated when calendar girl Kelly insisted she wanted full control of her wardrobe. Instead of beachwear, she was donning a strange array of 1940s-inspired dresses in a bid to look like Rita Hayworth. 'It's gutting that Kelly, who looks great in bikinis and made a career out of wearing them, won't put one on for a show which is set on a paradise island. She clearly wants to be seen as a Hollywood siren these days,' said one insider.

As the series somehow rolled on, there was unexpected resentment from the fans of *Coronation Street* when its regular slot was shifted to be shown an hour later on Monday evenings to make way for an attempted lead-in for *Love Island* in the hope of increased ratings. *Street* writers John Fay and Daran

Little complained bitterly to the press about the new schedule. Not that it did much good. ITV argued they had only moved Britain's longest-running and most popular soap when they deemed it absolutely necessary to do so to give the *Love Island* ratings a boost.

The objection was understandable. After all, it did seem that *Love Island* was just an excuse to throw together 12 non-A-list celebrities famed for their sexual behaviour and place them on a paradise island where viewers could – hopefully – see them copulate and vote on who they wanted to remove from the island. But it didn't quite work out like that. After a while, though, it did seem as if ITV's decision was the right one. The ratings began to pick up and at one point even beat *Big Brother* in the popularity stakes. Not that it had been smooth sailing by any means, and just when everything was looking up, the show was struck by another setback: this time a natural disaster and not a series of celebrity tantrums. On Friday, 10 June 2005 gale force storms raged over the islands of Fiji and disrupted the programme. A live eviction show had to be cancelled as unmanageable rough seas with six-foot waves made it impossible for crew members to cross over to where the celebrities were staying. Instead, ITV was forced to repeat the episode from the previous night with unseen footage.

If Fearne had already heard about the behind-the-scene dramas that had taken place during the making of the first series, it is perhaps surprising she ever agreed to co-host the programme's second outing one year after the first had been deemed such a flop. Perhaps that's why she was feeling a bit nervous about taking it on. But no, her reasons were different: 'I've never been on such an exposing show in a primetime slot every night. To step out from under that security blanket of my usual music shows is really exciting but obviously nerve-racking too. But it's a great chance to show that I'm not just about music or kids' TV.'

Probably her worst moment came at the show's end-of-series party when she was thrown fully clothed into a pool wearing a skimpy white dress that became completely transparent as soon as her body hit the water. Never one to bare herself, nude or semi-nude, she tried desperately to cover up when she realised what had happened. The crew were laughing but she took it all in good spirits. All the same, she was relieved when the dress dried quickly in the sun.

Not so amused by any of the events was online reviewer John Thorpe. In the conclusion of his write-up he could not help but say that the second series of *Love Island* was another awful television show. Costing upwards of £20 million, 'the show had come about after a table of executives held forth with hundreds of hopeful advertisers, drinking late into the afternoon, not writing or making creative choices, but hoping, praying, two marginally known individuals would have sex on the "people's channel". And chances are, even if that happens, they won't show it anyway.'

Neither did he think much of Fearne and Kielty, the programme's new presenters. Yes, they certainly enjoyed better chemistry than Kielty and Kelly Brook, but they were, in his opinion, still unsatisfying: 'Kielty can certainly read an autocue, but suffers from simply not being particularly funny or memorable. Meanwhile, Cotton's boundless enthusiasm and occasional hint of smuttiness is so commercially fulfilling, it reveals she surely can't care at all. *Love Island* was never charming or engrossing, or worth going back to, it was always tacky and offensive. Not standard offensive, of course, but offensive enough to those who waste their time watching it.'

All the same, it seemed as if Fearne had made quite a splash presenting *Love Island* with Kielty, despite the fact that the show still looked all washed-up in the ratings. The finale pulled in 3.8 million viewers, down 1.2 million on the previous year. It was indeed quite a change to the viewing figures bandied about in the 1980s when ITV regularly had half of Britain's TV audience watching its shows. In 1987, for example, an episode of *Coronation Street* attracted 26.6 million viewers. But at the time of *Love Island*, they had less than 20 per cent of the audience share.

So, the general consensus was shared with John Thorpe in that *Love Island* was, 'crass, dull, pointless, charmless, without merit – a programme that defines the range of soulless crap we're expected to sit down to. The worst show of the year.'

It was also unfortunate that the programme's poor ratings coincided with Charles Allen, the then chief executive of ITV, stepping down. Michael Grade, who took over that December, named *Love Island* among other high-profile flops of the time such as *It's Now or Never* with Phillip Schofield. One of the areas of most concern for Grade was that ITV 'have been very quick to copy other people's formats. We've stuck the word "celebrity" on the front of a copied format and pretended that's good enough. It is creatively bankrupt, to be honest, and we have got to wean ourselves off the habit.'

Nor did it help that ITV schedules at that time were packed with carbon copy shows. Even its Saturday-night hit *Dancing on Ice* was based on the BBC's *Strictly Come Dancing*. After losing Saturday-night viewers to the new *Doctor Who*, ITV responded with a time-travel monster show for family audiences, *Primeval*.

But it wasn't only ITV axing programmes from their schedules. After 42 years, the BBC also made the decision that it was time to end the show that Fearne loved presenting most of all … She was devastated.

Chapter 8

Radio Ga Ga

'I'm so excited about joining Radio 1. When I was a kid I did the classic thing of taping shows off the radio and dropping my own voice in.'

When *Top of the Pops* ended in July 2006, officially as a result of poor viewing figures, Fearne was still filming *Love Island* in Fiji, and was therefore not available to be in the *TOTP* studio for the last-ever broadcast of the show she so loved, and had described as her dream job. But all was not lost. Instead of missing out altogether, she recorded an introduction on location that could be transmitted at the start of the show.

As for the programme itself, this was pre-recorded on Wednesday, 26 July and shown on the following Sunday on BBC2. According to the BBC website, 'as the audience queued to get into the final recording of *Top of the Pops* there was something of a buzz in the air. Several people were dressed as their favourite pop stars and Axl Rose rubbed shoulders with Nana Mouskouri for possibly the first and last time. As the crowd entered the studio, decorated with logos from the past forty-two years of the BBC pop programme, the excitement only grew …' Of course the real question of the evening was: which bands will be appearing? The tickets promised 'surprise guests' and excited fans speculated they might see Robbie Williams, McFly or even the Rolling Stones close the show in much the same way as they had opened it, over four decades earlier.

In the end, they were to be disappointed. The last-ever *Top of the Pops* was constructed from archive performances and on the day they taped it with a live audience, the producers were merely recording the links between those clips. However, the crowd seemed to take it all in their stride, screaming for the cameras and singing along to a video of Sonny and Cher performing the epic 'I Got You Babe'. There was also excitement at seeing an eclectic array of presenters from the programme's history.

Sir Jimmy Savile, Janice Long, Dave Lee Travis and Tony Blackburn were back on the *Top of the Pops*' stage alongside more recent presenters such as Sarah Cawood and Reggie Yates. The guest presenters helped to keep the audience in high spirits, exchanging banter with the crowd and trading insults with one another.

At times it felt like a Radio 1 roadshow, as Sir Jimmy asked all the single women in the room to raise their hands. 'I haven't had so much fun since 1947,' exclaimed Tony Blackburn later in the recording. Others were less enthusiastic. 'My hair was black when we started this,' remarked the greying Dave Lee Travis. However, there was an air of nostalgia in the studio as classic moments from *Top of the Pops*' history were played out on big screens. 'It was sort of a trip down memory lane,' said Paul Cooksley, who was in the audience for the forty-fourth and final time. 'Watching some of the clips they were showing, I spotted some of the shows I'd been to in the past.'

Many of the elements that made *Top of the Pops* an institution in the 1970s were brought back for the programme's finale. A gigantic glitter ball hung from the ceiling, dry ice flooded the stage and dance troupe Pan's People made a fleeting appearance. As ever, the audience pushed and shoved for a spot beside the presenters in the hope of being seen on television back home. Those with deeley boppers, crazy wigs and short skirts were manoeuvred to the front by the show's ever-attentive floor managers. After a marathon two and a half hours, fireworks exploded and balloons dropped from the ceiling as the presenters read their final link. 'Perhaps we should say see you next week,' joked Mike Read.

But, as the studio lights went out, the carnival atmosphere gave way to a more sombre mood. The hosts huddled together to wonder whether the show would ever come back, while the production team took photographs of each other on the set for the last time. 'In twenty years' time we can say, "I was there",' said one member of the audience as they left the studio to the strains of Queen's 'We Are The Champions'. The whole atmosphere at the end 'was quite sad because everyone realised that that was it,' remarked Cooksley. 'It was obviously the end of an era and it was just really, really sad to have that brought to a close.'

But when the series was first launched in 1964, *Radio Times* announced that '*Top of the Pops*, a new series for teenagers, will be based on the latest discs, mainly hits from the current week's Top Twenty or Thirty. In many cases you will meet the artists whose records are being played; they will mime their songs. This is a departure from normal BBC practice, but the rule is being relaxed because the purpose of the programme is to let you hear the discs exactly as recorded, though within the setting of a television programme. No artist gives quite the same performance twice, but what goes out in *Top of the Pops* is precisely what won the "pop" in the first place.'

Forty years later, however, online reviewer Steve

Williams argued that no one has yet found a better way to present pop music on television: 'Certainly, no pop programmes nor, indeed, many programmes of all kinds, lasted longer than *Top of the Pops*, thanks to a format that is so simple and so effective that it almost seems bizarre that nobody had come up with it beforehand. Basically, it was the chart with pictures – thus guaranteeing that the viewer would hear their favourite songs and see their favourite pop stars.'

By the end of the 1990s, it seemed that virtually every channel had its own pop show. Some of them were hardly much of a threat. Five's *Pepsi Chart* was simply a lower-budget version of *Pops* and could normally only attract one or two live acts a week. But ITV's *CD:UK* was a different proposition entirely. Launched in August 1998, the show offered at least six live acts a week, an hour-long slot, a hyper audience and likeable presenters. Its biggest advantage, though, was how the scheduling on Saturday mornings was perfect for acts that wanted to convince the viewers to go out and buy their singles that afternoon, which of course resulted in bands clamouring to appear. It also counted down the Saturday Chart, which in reality was the midweek chart, before the official chart was issued the following day. Of course, this wasn't so accurate, but it still meant that it was a week ahead of *TOTP* and hence seemed much more up to date.

Making matters worse was when *Top of the Pops* was beaten in the ratings for one week in 1999 by, of all programmes, *Top of the Pops 2*. Williams correctly stated in his review of the last-ever *TOTP* that ever since its launch, the programme had progressed to becoming no more than a 'grab-bag of archive clips, along with the odd new video'. This unashamed nostalgia caused an increase in viewing figures and meant that the programme was moved from Saturday afternoons to an early evening Wednesday slot. *Pops'* little BBC2 sister gained a couple of hundred thousand viewers and now seemed a better platform for new acts; Eva Cassidy and the Mavericks made their first TV appearances on the show and this was cited as the reason for an increase in their record sales.

The BBC, at least outwardly, still supported the series. In October 2001 the show moved from Elstree studios, where it had been based for the previous decade, which proved inconvenient for acts and audiences – and made it one of the last BBC-produced programmes not to be broadcast in widescreen – and returned to BBC Television Centre. The new location was home to the Star Bar, as well as a dedicated studio. This allowed the public to see celebrity guests off-duty and enjoy a little more showbiz glamour. But the main problem was that it was a working bar, not a TV studio, so any celebrity chat was drowned out by the background noise.

In early 2003 the number of acts on the show was reduced in favour of more behind-the-scenes material and feature items, a somewhat pointless decision, it seemed, especially as behind-the-scenes footage was often repetitive. After six months this was abandoned when Chris Cowey left the programme (and the BBC) to return to freelance work. In his place came a former presenter Andi Peters. Famous for his work in the *Broom Cupboard*, Peters started to make waves behind the scenes, at LWT and in his most recent appointment as Head of Youth Programmes at Channel 4, where he came up with the concept for *T4*. Now he was back at the Corporation as editor of pop programmes.

Initially, *Top of the Pops* was unchanged – indeed, the Star Bar was closed down and the series returned to its original format of featuring nothing but performances. Yet this was only a temporary measure while Peters planned a radical revamp, which would turn out to be the biggest change for over a decade. As his starting point he took the idea that, with numerous channels pumping out back-to-back videos, *Top of the Pops* needed to be doing something more than stringing performances together, which was too passive an experience for today's viewers. There was some merit in the idea, but the question was whether this was suitable for a programme that went out on Friday nights when a sizeable number of the audience had one eye on the screen and the other on choosing an outfit for their big night out.

Nevertheless, Peters's revamp, which came into force on 28 November 2003, was so radical it was announced that the programme would now be officially known as *All New Top of the Pops*. A brand new set was built and the series returned to being broadcast live, something that hadn't happened since All About Eve memorably failed to hear their backing track in 1988. A full-time presenter was also booked – MTV host Tim Kash.

Increasingly studio performances were now interspersed with competitions, interviews, phone-ins and features. The old style of feature where a camera would follow Busted to the canteen in the hope that they'd say something funny no longer appeared, but instead special reports followed pop stars, in the studio or on tour. It was a packed programme and therefore the number of live acts dropped from eight to nearer five or six.

Unfortunately the new format proved unsuccessful. Generally, features were extremely dull – it was hard to see how the mass audience would be spellbound by the sight of Lostprophets wandering round an airport, or someone called Christina Christian presenting the dullest of news from the American chart in a monotone. Presenter Kash turned out to be something of an acquired taste, unable to display much personality, while

Above left: Gunged on the set of the game show *Pump It Up* alongside co-host Andy Collins.

Above right: Fooling around with *Finger Tips* co-presenter Stephen Mulhern.

Below left: Attending the *Jackass* film premiere, February 2003.

Below right: Preparing to take part in Cancer Research UK's Race For Life campaign, May 2003.

Fearne does *Celebrity Fame Academy*. Pictured here alongside her fellow competitors (*above*) and after her final performance (*below left*).

© *PA Photos*

Below right: Attending the British Academy Children's Film and Television Awards, London, November 2003.

© *REX Features*

Fearne and her former boyfriend, hell-raising *Fame Academy* contestant Peter Brame.

Above left: Snapped in the back of a taxi with Lostprophets frontman Ian Watkins – the next day the pair went public with their relationship.

Above right: Launching *Serious Arctic*, a new children's wildlife show for the BBC, January 2005.

Below: Fearne and Kermit the Frog on *Holly and Stephen's Saturday Showdown*.

© *REX Features*

Chilling out at V2004 Festival in Weston Park.

Above: With fellow Radio 1 presenter Edith Bowman at the Tsunami Relief concert in Cardiff, January 2005.

© *PA Photos*

Always game for a laugh, Fearne is frequently featured on various weekend game shows. She's been seen hurtling across the studio in a rocket on *Ant and Dec's Saturday Night Takeaway* (*below left*) and shrieking hysterically as her and Holly Willoughby are soaked with cold water on *Holly and Stephen's Saturday Showdown* (*below right*).

© *REX Features*

Above left: With Chris Parker, one of her best mates.

Above right and below: Having a laugh in Fiji whilst co-presenting ITV's *Love Island* with Irish star Patrick Kielty.

Fearne with her new beau, American part-time model, Jesse Jenkins.

Peters simply booked ancient acts such as Elton John and Sting. Reports also stated that all these extra features had spiralled the programme way over budget.

Inevitably changes were made – the number of features scaled down (though never completely dropped during this era) and Kash began to rotate his stints as presenter with Fearne and Reggie Yates before his contract failed to be renewed after its first year. There was also an increased number of attention-grabbing stunts, with performances taking place on the roof or in the car park of Television Centre; one entire episode in July 2004 was broadcast live from Newcastle. Yet no matter how many new ideas were pioneered, the fact that the programme continued to be broadcast opposite *Coronation Street* meant viewing figures failed to increase to any great extent.

This couldn't go on, and eventually a big decision was finally taken: *Top of the Pops* would no longer be broadcast on BBC1 and instead was to become a fully fledged BBC2 series from July 2005. There was also to be a new time slot, with the show now broadcast on Sunday evenings, which was at least fairly sensible as it meant that the programme would go out just five minutes after the new chart had been revealed, rather than five days later. Thought was also given to how it might all appeal to a more BBC2 audience, which would be done by merging the programme with *Top of the*

Pops 2 and pairing existing host Fearne with a new guest each week to add a different perspective.

With the features now abandoned, the new BBC2 *Top of the Pops* was back to straight performances, with one or two archive clips. Often the guest hosts were in direct contrast to the slick pop presenters, with personalities such as Jeremy Clarkson, Sue Barker and news reporter Jeremy Bowen all taking a turn. The odd notable choice aside – obviously Clarkson slagging off most of the acts – willing co-hosts were not so easy to find and most weeks familiar faces such as Richard Bacon and Phill Jupitus took a turn, simply hosting the show in the way that the Radio 1 DJs would have done in the past.

Although because of its new slot, the programme could reveal the latest chart for the first time on TV, this often had a detrimental effect – bands needed to be booked way ahead, and in between the booking and their appearance they might find themselves entering low down the chart or even missing the Top 40 altogether. Worse still, because the series was now on BBC2, with smaller audiences of between one and two million viewers, some of the bigger names were disinclined to make an appearance – so while the format was probably just as good as in previous years, the quality of the acts was poorer.

Early in the BBC2 run, Andi Peters quit the show to return to presenting, with Mark Cooper taking over as executive producer. Cooper was head of all contemporary music programming at the BBC, originating such classics as *Later with Jools Holland*, and it was hard to see how someone from the serious end of music television would have an equal enthusiasm for a series that still had its roots very much in light entertainment.

Finally, on 20 June 2006, it was announced that *Top of the Pops* was to come to an end. In an era of continuous TV music, and with the market splintered into umpteen genres, the BBC claimed there was no call for a half-hour programme of this type and they were keen to point out that it certainly didn't mean the end for pop music on the BBC, with occasional editions of *Top of the Pops 2*, featuring some new material, and a regular series of live pop concerts going out under the name of *The BBC1 Sessions*.

Although Fearne wasn't present at the taping of the last *TOTP* at Television Centre to see the show out, she didn't appear to mourn for long and remained her upbeat self. It seemed she had enjoyed filming in Fiji just as much as she had done presenting *Top of the Pops*: 'I can safely say that doing *Love Island* was the best three months of my life. Living in Fiji, it felt like I had no responsibilities. All I had to do was get up, go to work and lie on the beach. It doesn't bother me that the ratings were bad – there's always going to be another project that I can get my teeth into. Hopefully, if I keep working hard, there will be new stuff to replace the ones that don't come back.'

And one of those projects that could perhaps be seen to replace *Love Island* was already waiting in the wings by the time she flew back. It was while ITV were actually in the throes of axing *Love Island* for good that they came up with the idea of Fearne doing a new dating show with her best friend and presenter Holly Willoughby. It was decided the pair would style themselves as the Trinny and Susannah of the dating world as they set about fixing the love lives of the six singletons to appear in the show each week.

Similarly, Fearne was also hoping to fix her own love life. Before jetting off to Fiji, she had been to Los Angeles where a mate introduced her to a guy named Jesse Jenkins, a sometime model and wannabe chef. When she first set eyes on him, she couldn't believe her luck: 'I immediately thought, "Who's *that?*" I was like: "God, he's gorgeous!" We had a snog and knew we fancied each other. But then I didn't see him all summer because I was in Fiji filming.'

Although the first months of their relationship were spent apart, that didn't stop the couple from calling each other and texting regularly. But it was only when Fearne went back out to LA after she had finished work on *Love Island* that she realised, 'We still fancied each other, so we hung out a bit and realised it was serious.' She also knew that she couldn't be without Jesse. Eventually, to her delight he made the decision to come over to Britain to live.

He wasn't living in Britain full-time but as Fearne explained, 'He was staying here a lot and then goes back to America for a little bit.' All the same, she was pleased: 'It doesn't put any pressure on us because I'm so busy right now.' And when *Cosmopolitan* magazine caught up with her for a July 2007 feature, she was happy to admit that she hadn't slept in her own bed for about two months.

According to Holly Willoughby, 'They are the prettiest, coolest couple in the world.' But marriage wasn't something that was on their minds. According to Fearne, she and Jesse are in a great place as they are. If anything, she confesses, 'I'm probably a rather loud and annoying girlfriend. Jesse always has a go at me for telling him the same story five times. But he's really romantic, always leaving me notes and things.' So whenever she is asked if he's the one, she admits that she hopes so, yes.

Even today, they are still very much together and in love. If the suggestion that Jesse left his home country and moved to London just for her is true, then, 'Er, well, yes he did,' admits Fearne. 'But we're both people who like spontaneous, exciting things and if you fall in love, you're going to be miserable if you're not with that person. We go back to America all the time so he's not away for that long a stretch.'

'He's my toy boy. I know, it's terrible!' she screeches, more than happy with the situation. 'I'm 25 and he's 21, but in ten years' time, that won't even be a gap. We have the same dreams, and that's what counts. He's definitely the most wonderful, delightful boy I've met in my whole life.'

Just over a year since they met, they went camping with friends to Cornwall: 'When we arrived it was pissing with rain, the wind was howling, and quite frankly, I wanted to cry. But instead I let my boyfriend put the tent up and poured myself a wine. After this, to prove even further that they were, in fact, men, all the boys ran into the sea. It was freezing, unappealing and rough, but for some reason they all loved it! The next day was gorgeous and we spent the rest of the trip eating pasties and fudge, drinking wine, BBQing (even when raining), walking on the beach, telling stories round the fire in a rather clichéd way and sleeping in awkward positions. It was a blast! You really can't beat camping.' Her advice to other would-be campers was to camp it up, have a ball and take more socks than you think you need: 'My toes didn't belong to me most mornings!'

Apart from being 'loved-up', as she described it, that same year, towards the end of September, she was also given a new opportunity at Radio 1 when she was taken on to co-present the weekend breakfast show with Reggie Yates. The pair had been doing the early morning show on Friday mornings from 4 till 7, so the new programme was, for Fearne, another dream come true. Already she had been over the moon about the early morning gig for the station and so the new weekend show was simply the icing on the cake. When she first joined Radio 1, she said, 'I'm looking forward to talking about music, obsessing about music and playing loads of music. I'm so excited about joining Radio 1. When I was a kid I did the classic thing of taping shows off the radio and dropping my own voice in. Hopefully this show will be better than that!'

Yates commented, 'It'll be brilliant – Fearne and I are proper mates and we both have a genuine love of music.' This was reinforced when a Radio 1 spokesman welcomed the move: 'Reggie and Fearne are really hot at the moment and I'm chuffed they are ready to get up early to do this show. It'll be an ultimate guide to what to do at the weekend and as they are passionate about different types of new music, love going to different gigs and generally having a good time, it should make for some great radio.'

Reggie, of course, had by this time established himself as one of the most talented and versatile young performers and presenters on British television. Already he had followed Fearne on to *Comic Relief Does Fame*

Academy and of course he had been her regular stablemate on *Top of the Pops*. Although he had appeared in some dramas for CBBC, notably *Grange Hill* and *UGetMe*, presenting gigs was what he enjoyed the most. Aside from the *Reg & Dev* show that he did for Radio 1's sister station 1Xtra, he also sat in for major players such as Trevor Nelson in much the same way as Fearne had done for Sara Cox.

Of course, the new weekend show was an integral part of an already star-studded weekend daytime schedule featuring Vernon Kay, Sara Cox, Trevor Nelson and Radio 1's *Chart Show* with JK and Joel. Again, Fearne was as enthusiastic as ever: 'I'm over the moon about Reggie and I getting this new show on Radio 1. I've had a fantastic time so far and know that it's just going to get even better.' And again Reggie couldn't help but agree: 'Being a part of the weekend team at Radio 1 is really exciting; there is definitely a family feel at the station and I'm ready to meet the weekend in-laws!'

As far as Ben Cooper, then head of Mainstream Radio at the BBC was concerned, he could not have been more pleased: 'This is a key show for Radio 1 and Fearne and Reggie are total stars. I believe we now have the best weekend line-up in music radio in the country.'

Fearne and Reggie were, in fact, taking over from Spoony, who had decided to try something new. As he himself said at the time, 'I've had a fantastic six years at

Radio 1, it's a brilliant place to work and has been amazing for my career. I'm going to miss the listeners and the wonderful back-room team that I worked with – they made getting up at a ridiculous time of the weekend that little bit easier. But I'm now really looking forward to getting my teeth stuck into my role at Five Live, where I get to share my passions for sport and broadcasting. I have a number of very exciting broadcasting irons in the fire and now, leaving Radio 1 on a high, I can explore some of the offers I have on the table.'

DJ Spoony departed from the station when the weekend breakfast show was high on listening figures with a loyal audience, which, in turn, provided Fearne and Reggie with quite an act to follow. In much the same way, one year later, they took over the *Chart Show* from JK and Joel after three and a half years of presenting one of the most listened-to programmes on Radio 1.

Of course for many over the age of forty, the *Chart Show* really began with the BBC Light Programme in 1962 when *Pick of the Pops,* then simply a singles chart countdown presented by DJ and radio personality Alan 'Fluff' Freeman, was given a regular Sunday teatime slot. It became a national institution and continued to be one of the most listened-to programmes when Radio 1 launched in 1967. Although Freeman presented the show for the next five years, he eventually left the BBC in favour of commercial radio. In many ways, he was a pioneer of British radio, the *Chart Show* and the disc jockey. In those days, the lively, modern presentation style he introduced was still relatively obscure when you consider that before he came on to the scene the best listeners could expect was a typically upper-class BBC broadcaster stiffly announcing such lines as 'that was the new gramophone record sung by Frank Sinatra'.

According to a later *Chart Show* host, Richard Skinner, *Pick of the Pops* was the absolute flagship show. 'Younger people now perhaps wouldn't appreciate just how dominant it was,' agreed David Jensen, who in 1984 launched the rival *Network Chart* on commercial radio, combining sales and airplay. (From 1 August 1993, Neil Fox took over the rebranded *Pepsi Network Chart*, which later became the *Pepsi Chart* and then *hit40uk*.) Even though Skinner can remember joking about how Jensen was playing the same records in a different order, 'Clearly what he was doing was the beginning of a change.'

That change was commercial radio, which, quite naturally, capitalised on the so-called unsettled times at Radio 1 in the mid-1990s, when controversial changes saw the departure of several veteran deejays (Simon Bates, Tony Blackburn, Tommy Vance, Mark Goodier and Bruno Brookes), and this in turn gave more elbow to the commercial stations. 'We were a personality chart that was a really fun show, with competitions, interviews with the stars making the hits and montage recaps,' recalls Neil Fox, who took over the *Network Chart* in 1993. 'If you listened to JK and Joel on Radio 1, it's everything the *Pepsi Chart* was ten years ago.'

Indeed, the audience for the commercial radio chart eventually outdid Radio 1. This was something that Mark Goodier, another BBC *Chart Show* presenter, found unfortunate:'That was a very sad era when the chart was not a priority for Radio 1, and when they had considered taking it off the air, they opened the door to the commercial radio chart gaining in strength. In the end it was on more than a hundred stations.' Fox, however, was not a fan of *hit40uk*, the show that replaced his own: 'They ruined the whole thing; they thought they needed to change for the sake of it and Radio 1 now has the biggest chart again.' Just as Fearne and Reggie were announced to be taking over from JK and Joel – this couldn't have been better timing, had Fearne planned the whole thing herself.

Equally interesting is the chart itself. The first British singles chart was published in the 14 November 1952 edition of the *New Musical Express* (*NME*). It was, initially, little more than a gimmick, a tool in the circulation war against *NME*'s much older and more popular rival, *Melody Maker*.

Intriguingly enough, to start with the chart was only

a Top 12, and was indeed the creation of the paper's advertising manager, Percy Dickins, who compiled it by calling around some 20 major record stores and aggregating their sales reports. He continued personally to oversee the compilation method well into the 1960s. Although the chart rapidly became one of the paper's most popular features, it also grew to be a stable for record labels to quote in almost every pop advert and press release they put out. Nor did it take long for Britain's other major music papers to jump on the bandwagon with their own version. One of them was *Record Mirror* and another, not surprisingly, was *Melody Maker*.

The forerunner to the official chart first came about, however, from the industry trade publication *Record Retailer*, now *Music Week*, who in 1960 printed a weekly Top 50 that was not immediately recognised as an official listing. Arguably, the *NME* chart was still the most recognised, no doubt helped by the fact that it was used as the official chart on Radio Luxembourg, then one of the most listened-to radio stations.

As the 1960s rolled on, it seemed as if there wasn't a single publication that wasn't striving to have their chart recognised as the correct one. Of course all this led to some very interesting historical anomalies. The Beatles' second single, for instance, 'Please Please Me' was Number One on most charts, but not in *Record Retailer*.

Adding to the confusion was the method in which the chart used by the BBC on *Pick of the Pops* was actually calculated by averaging out all the other charts; it was as if no one agreed.

It wasn't until 1969 that a reliable and officially recognised chart emerged, through an alliance between the BBC and *Record Retailer*. For the first time, a professional polling organisation, BMRB, was commissioned to oversee the chart from a pool of 500 record shops across Britain, more than twice as many as had been used for any previous compilation of the week's bestsellers. That was when an official Top 50 was inaugurated, which by 1978 expanded into a Top 75.

Matters became even more complicated in 1982, a year after Fearne was born, when BMRB lost their contract to Gallup, who subsequently arranged to gather electronic data to replace the old sales diary method of compiling an accurate chart. The first chart terminals appeared in record shops two years later and, as a result, by the autumn of 1987 it was then possible for the chart, incorporating sales up to close of business on Saturday, to be announced on Sunday afternoon rather than being delayed until the following Tuesday, as had previously happened.

All the same, Reggie was just pleased that he and Fearne had been asked to host a show that most presenters would probably have loved to have got their hands on: 'It's really exciting to be a part of the chart as new music is what we are all about and it doesn't get much better than announcing the new Number One!' Fearne couldn't agree more. The fact that she was now the first-ever regular female presenter in history for the UK Top 40 was simply a bonus: 'I can't wait to start the new show with Reg on Radio 1. Announcing the chart each week will be so exciting.' She was also looking forward to the request show that they had been given to host on Saturday mornings.

This was all part of a major revamp to focus on the under-eighteens that included the recruitment of Kelly Osbourne as a presenter while JK and Joel were out of a job. Under the new schedule, the Chris Moyles breakfast show was increased by another half-hour and Osbourne became the new host of *The Surgery*, all part of the new 'teen zone' on Sunday evenings that introduced another new show hosted by Annie Mac. Friday nights focused on dance music and Saturday nights were all about urban music. Fearne and Reggie hosted the *Chart Show* and a new audience request show.

Nihal DJed the weekend breakfast show and TV duo Dick and Dom were drafted in for a new Sunday morning show while former student DJ Greg James took on the early breakfast slot. 'It's important that we keep up the change of pace and innovation, both on air and online,' said Andy Parfitt, controller of Radio 1, 1Xtra and

Teens. 'This simplifies and strengthens Radio 1 and is an important step in providing programmes focused on the under-eighteen audience. The Sunday evening line-up, which I'm delighted includes Kelly Osbourne, is a great addition to a zone that will include Fearne, Reggie and Annie. The new Radio 1 schedule, coupled with the recently announced changes for 1Xtra, really gives us the chance of turbo-charging the BBC's performance with young audiences over the coming years.'

Not that online critic Elisabeth Mahoney entirely agreed. If anything, she was convinced radio audiences are notoriously resistant to change and therefore wondered how listeners would react to the clutch of changes in presenter line-ups Radio 1 had made. If her review on *Guardian Unlimited* was anything to go by, this wasn't good news. On a first listen, she thought the *Chart Show* had, 'come over all gossipy and frantic now that Fearne and Reggie have taken over. Has anyone ever sounded less sincere than Fearne Cotton rambling on about what great guys the Hoosiers are, and how her New Year's resolution is to hang out with them?' It was, Mahoney said, 'an odd thing to say in October' three months before the New Year had started. But then again, perhaps Fearne and Reggie just weren't her kind of presenters.

Among those who agreed to differ was Ben Cooper: 'In the year that Radio 1 celebrates 40 years of bringing new music to its audience I believe we are now delivering the best schedule possible. We've made it simpler and even easier for our audience to navigate, which is key in such a crowded media world. The line-up allows us to nurture new talent and at the same time have the biggest DJs in terms of both music and entertainment on the station – it's a total package for our audience to enjoy and, for me, represents public service at its best.' And he was probably right.

Chapter 9

Cotton Candy Land

'So much has changed in the decade since I started out. I wanted to be an actress, then a presenter. Fame didn't come into it. I do find it terrifying now that someone wins a reality show and is famous the next day.'

Twenty-four hours before she was due to arrive in Los Angeles to host the *Oscars Red Carpet Live* for Sky One in February 2007, Fearne had just got back from a workout at her local gym in south-west London. Her sink was full of washing-up and she was wearing an old red tracksuit, sports socks and a 'disgusting sports bra that has gone all grey in the wash'. Her front room floor was covered in a blizzard of files, paperwork and books, including her current read: Leonardo DiCaprio's biography.

She still couldn't quite believe her luck that soon she would be interviewing the stars as they arrived for the 79th Academy Awards on what is the most important day of Hollywood's calendar: the Oscars Ceremony. Early that morning, the Los Angeles Police Department had been putting up barricades and cordoning off streets. With billions' worth of movie stardom arriving in just a few hours time, they were taking no risks with security. By midday the sniffer dogs used by the Bomb Squad had done their job around the 3,000-seater auditorium and plain-clothes detectives scanned the faces of the fans for that one star-crazed lunatic or terrorist who might want to claim his or her five minutes of fame.

Fearne, however, was just excited to be attending the event, a gig most movie buffs would give their right arm for: 'Wearing a gorgeous frock, chatting to all the movie stars and watching all the glamour of the red carpet will be amazing,' she raved. 'And the possibility of seeing Johnny Depp in the flesh is mind-blowingly brilliant! I'm looking forward to bringing back all the gossip.'

This was why she had been spending the last few weeks absorbing everything there was to know about such stars as Johnny Depp, Leonardo DiCaprio and Kate Winslet, while her personal stylist was out combing the designer rails for a dress that would look appropriate:

very Oscarish but still practical. After all, as she laughed, 'I don't want to upstage Cate Blanchett!'

Not that she would have much of a chance. She would only be on the red carpet outside the Kodak Theater in downtown Los Angeles for 90 minutes before the ceremony began and already the stars would be seated inside the now-permanent home of the Oscars, waiting for their host, stand-up comedienne and actress Ellen DeGeneres, to start the proceedings. That was all the time she had been given to get the gen on how the guests and nominees were feeling, which performances impressed them the most and, naturally, what they were all wearing.

For Fearne, things could not have been better when Helen Mirren, who collected the Best Actress Award for her leading performance in Stephen Frears's *The Queen*, posed with the Union Jack that she had snatched away from Fearne and waved it around proudly. One cannot imagine any other actor or actress doing such a thing without agonising whether their actions might be construed as too yobbish or partisan.

Neither could Fearne. Although she was pleased to have seen it all up close, she admits to this day that the Oscars was the most chaotic mayhem she has ever experienced: 'I had exactly one metre of red carpet and was penned in next to Ryan Seacrest and a very loud American lady to the right of me. I hardly remember a thing as you just get thrown movie stars, minute after minute. Let me tell you, I needed one large gin after!'

Of course that was before she had gone teetotal three months before the end of the year. Now she would much prefer to settle down with a nice cup of tea without any sugar. Not very rock'n'roll, she admits, but then again, on the whole she has always been careful not to be seen in any embarrassing pap shots looking the worse for wear. That's not to say she doesn't like partying but she usually does this when she goes to gigs and it's still one of her favourite things to do when she isn't working.

As Mary Riddell noted in the *Daily Mail*, while Fearne is very pretty, 'the glamour queens of Hollywood are unlikely to be eclipsed by a twenty-four-year-old reality TV show presenter with a taste for vintage chiffon and "Mum, Dad and Jamie" tattooed on her neck'. In many ways, she is still regarded as a 'homely young woman who has always steered her way carefully around drink, drugs and self-destruction, she is also flamboyant enough to stand out among an army of hopefuls who dream of being her'.

Not that her confidence has been damaged in any way because of comments in the press. Nor has she been concerned that she might be, as some journalists have said, the Jonah of celebrity broadcasting. 'Besides TV is always changing,' she says. 'People want to see new and exciting things. I've no regrets about doing anything. *Love Island* was the best time of my life – wonderful, peaceful and brilliant. It's a shame it's not coming back, but it was a good springboard for me.'

As anyone who has ever met Fearne will make a point of telling you, she seems genuinely nice but she is equally serious about her career. It's the kind of self-drilled discipline she has instilled in herself since childhood to overcome any obstacles that may have got in the way: 'I have such an odd position here, being in the public eye all the time. We have a bitchy media, with magazines running stories saying, "Doesn't she look fat? Doesn't she look terrible?"'

It is one of the reasons why she is not eager to expose herself too much to scrutiny. Such reticence seems odd, though. Surely a former presenter of *Love Island* should, in theory, be a prime evangelist for celebrity culture at its most tawdry, and anyone who claims, as she has, that her heroine is Davina McCall can never be accused of being overtly highbrow. Nonetheless, she is startlingly averse to the terrifying dangers now facing young girls: 'So much has changed in the decade since I started out,' she continues. 'I wanted to be an actress, then a presenter. Fame didn't come into it. I do find it terrifying now that someone wins a reality show and is famous the next day. Maybe that will last a year, maybe not, and then they're recognised in public, which is the annoying bit, without any job to back it up. It's terrifying that people equate fame with success. You can be extremely famous without having any training or income and I find that frightening.'

Although she loved reality television – and working for it – the unhealthy bit, she says, 'is how some magazines put celebrity across as a super-glamorous life without telling girls that there's no substance to such fame; it's crazy. I'm terrified at the thought of young girls looking at pictures of skinny models and thinking they must be like that. They have no energy, they're depressed, but magazines make out that thin equals happy – it's all, "Look at her, she's so horrible and fat".'

As the presenter of Channel Five's *Make Me A Supermodel*, she probably understood that more than most. Julia Robson, writing in the *Daily Telegraph*, noted: 'The reality TV show has been a surprise ratings hit. It follows the tried-and-tested *Pop Idol* format, but the contestants are more beautiful, and the Simon Cowell role is played by the altogether more glamorous, but no less outspoken Rachel Hunter.'

When the show started, 13 lucky young girls were plucked from thousands of wannabe models and installed in a luxurious, *Big Brother*-style house in Richmond, Surrey. Three times a week over a fortnight the viewers got to know the girls as they were put through very real and often unsavoury fashion industry tasks, including a photographic shoot (where they were encouraged to strip off) and a trip to New York, where they were kept awake for 48 hours.

The judges were Tandy Anderson (a tough, former Mary Quant model, who co-founded the Select model agency that discovered Helena Christensen and Sienna Miller), Perou (an outspoken magazine photographer, who hides behind enormous, dark-framed glasses) and Hunter, who rarely smiles and whose criticisms of the would-be models verge on the surreal, when she told one contestant, for example, that she was 'morbid'.

In each episode, the judges picked a girl to be eliminated but not before she was told why, in their view, she was not cut out for the glamorous fashion life. 'Skin was bad, end of story,' said one judge when Katie Black, a beautiful 21-year-old from Paisley, was the first model to be kicked off the show. 'Plain,' said another, dismissively.

The girls, some as young as 17, were regularly reduced to tears. They were told they were eating too much, or not enough; their looks were criticised, their personalities dissected. Among other things they were called 'drab', 'tarty', 'boring' and 'cry-babies'. To top it all, the cameras followed them back to their temporary home, where they all but clawed one another's eyes out. 'Of course modelling *is* bitchy,' said Tandy. 'It's because it's so competitive – it brings out the worst in everyone.'

171

Viewers may well have wondered why on earth anyone would choose to work in such a cruel industry. Who would want to be treated like dirt by photographers and agents? On one edition of the show, Julia Robson was reminded of her own past when the programme returned to haunt her: 'A few days ago, I was asked to be a panellist on the show, charged with finding out from the would-be models why they thought they deserved to be an ambassador for the Italian superbrand MaxMara.

'As the three remaining finalists, Joanna Downes, Kate Ellery and Alice Sinclair, entered the room on wobbly high heels, my heart suddenly lurched. I was reminded of the time I found myself – as a gawky 17-year-old model – in a poky Tokyo apartment, which was filled to bursting point with hormonal, homesick girls. We were all competing to win a contract with a London agency that had a branch in Japan (I came second). My time in Tokyo was the most nerve-racking but fascinating experience I had ever had. Every month, the models were weighed in front of one another. If we put on weight, the booker would dock our monthly allowance.

'I learnt very quickly that looks are only a small part of what you need to succeed as a model. You need to be tough enough to cope with the many weird situations you're likely to find yourself in – for me, that included doing an underwear shoot halfway up Mount Fuji in the

172

middle of winter, and dressing up as a tomato for a roadside poster campaign.'

But, of course, she continues, 'some things have changed since my day. When I made my debut, twenty years ago, as a cover girl for *Jackie* magazine – I know, hardly *Vogue* – the fellow models who took me under their wings and dragged me to nightclubs were mostly frightfully posh Lucie Clayton types. Today, girls from all backgrounds can make it in the industry – if they've got the right level of mental toughness.

'The scariest thing about modelling today is how quickly you can get to the top – that shocks me,' says Tandy Anderson. 'It used to take years to reach certain levels and there was always a healthy hierarchy. Now, in a flash, you can go from nothing to being enormous.'

The girl tipped to win the top prize – a contract with Select – was Kate, an A-level student from a very ordinary background in south Wales, who works in a café at weekends. 'Kate has made it on personality and quirkiness; she's a great all-rounder,' agreed Tandy. 'The three finalists have grasped the most important skills – they now know there's much more to being a successful, modern-day model than having a pretty face.'

Even with her well-balanced vegetarian diet and size 10 figure, one cannot help but wonder if Fearne's passionate aversion to the darker side of celebrity suggests that she too has been affected by all the pressure. Perhaps she has, because her rise to prominence is still a curious one, considering her mixed history.

Before the Oscars, she had covered the *Brit Awards*, and one month after the Oscars she played a major role in *Comic Relief* and *Making Your Mind Up*, the programme and competition to pick Britain's Eurovision Song Contest entry, which interestingly enough was plunged into a farce when she and Terry Wogan shouted out different winners at the same time, forcing red-faced BBC chiefs to apologise after they received more than a hundred complaints about the voting blunder: 'It seems clear that most viewers have appreciated that this was a genuine mistake. These things can happen in live television and the mix-up was immediately corrected so there was no harm done. We would like to sincerely apologise to viewers for the confusion when announcing the winner.'

The actual winners (revealed by Fearne) were a camp foursome known as Scooch, with their airline-themed 'Flying The Flag (For You)', but Wogan announced to the nation that French singer Cyndi had won the viewer's vote. Two days later he insisted he wasn't to blame for announcing the wrong winner on the night in question. He told his Radio 2 listeners that French singer Cyndi had won, but seconds later Fearne confirmed that Scooch were the victors: 'Nobody died, it wasn't the

General Election and people got a bit confused. I suppose I should make a little apology to Cyndi, although I'm not taking the blame for this because I was the one who did say Cyndi had won. And if she's listening, my apologies for raising your hopes at the last minute, which was inadvertent and I'm sorry.'

But Cyndi didn't seem to think Wogan *was* at fault. She said, 'He's human and we all make mistakes. He didn't need to apologise. Not for one second have I felt even a little bit of embarrassment and I wasn't at all mad or upset.' Making matters worse was when the BBC claimed it was indeed Wogan's mistake. And that was reinforced when a BBC spokesperson said, 'Terry was given the right name down his earpiece. There was no technical problem. It was noisy in the studio so he could have misheard but he was definitely given the right name.'

However, there were no such misunderstandings when the Eurovision Song Contest was held in Helsinki, Finland in May of that year and Fearne returned to European television screens as the face for the United Kingdom vote despite having to announce that the highest award of 12 points went to Turkey, not Britain.

The Eurovision Song Contest wasn't the only time when she would work with Wogan. Six months after Helsinki she was again on hand to help him present *Children In Need* for the usual evening of fun, interspersed with a host of heartstring-tugging tales. She still had fond memories of the programme she did the year before when McFly kicked things off at 7.00pm, followed by the apprentices from *Celebrity Scissorhands*, who had been practising on the public all week and were let loose to give a host of stars, including the cast of *Hollyoaks,* a makeover.

Other surreal highlights include *Holby City*'s doctors and nurses swapping scrubs for spandex to perform Madonna's 'Hung Up', domestic goddesses Kim and Aggie hitting the road with Status Quo to find out *How Clean Is Your Gig?*. And the BBC newsreaders (who always throw themselves into the spirit of things) presented their unique tribute to 007. Pleasing Fearne, no end, there was plenty of live music throughout the five-hour show from Girls Aloud, the Sugababes, Bradley Walsh, Richard Fleeshman, Amy Winehouse, Keane, Nelly Furtado, Ronan Keating, James Morrison and Lemar, as well as the official *Children In Need* song, which that year was 'Downtown', originally made famous by Petula Clark and performed by Spice Girl Emma Bunton and the stars of *Strictly Come Dancing*.

And, of course, Fearne's own personal favourite highlight from 2003 was when she appeared in the music video for the official *Children In Need* single, 'I'm Your Man', originally recorded by *EastEnders*' star Shane Richie and released under the name of Wham! Fearne

176

made her appearance as the barmaid that Shane flirts with at the Club Tropicana bar.

Interestingly enough, the first BBC broadcast appeal for children was a five-minute radio programme on Christmas Day in 1927. It raised £1,143 18s 3d and the proceeds were shared with four prominent children's charities. And the first televised appeal was in 1955 when *Children's Hour Christmas Appeal*, presented by Sooty and Harry Corbett, was launched. The Christmas Day appeals continued on TV and radio right up until 1979, raising a total of £625,836. Among the presenters were Terry Hall, Eamonn Andrews, Leslie Crowther, Michael Aspel and the then rising star of the Radio 2 Breakfast Show, Terry Wogan, who made his debut appearance in 1978.

In 1980 the appeal was broadcast on BBC1 in a new telethon format, hosted by Wogan with Sue Lawley and Esther Rantzen. The telethon captured the public's imagination to such an extent that the donations increased dramatically and broke the £1 million mark for the very first time.

Pudsey made his television debut in 1985 when Wogan introduced the new, brown cuddly mascot to the audience. He was designed by BBC graphic designer Joanna Ball, who named him after the West Yorkshire town where she had been born. The bear proved very popular, and the following year, he returned as *Children*

In Need's official logo with his design amended to that of a yellow bear with a red-spotted bandage.

In the two decades that followed, countless cuddly bears have been sold to raise money for the charity, while Pudsey himself has received letters, drawings and emails from youngsters all over the UK and been photographed with more celebrities than he can remember. Apart from a party hat worn in 2004 to celebrate the telethon's silver jubilee, Pudsey's image has remained much the same, but a 2007 revamp has given him a fresh new look and brighter colours in readiness for what became, quite surprisingly, the twenty-eighth annual BBC *Children In Need* appeal.

Of course, the annual telethon continues to this day and also remains a highlight of the charity's year-long campaign when the whole BBC joins together to support BBC *Children In Need* on TV, radio and online. The live show features some of the fundraising activities taking place around the UK, as well as unexpected performances from familiar faces. Terry Wogan remains the telethon's mainstay and he has been joined by a diverse line-up over the years that includes Joanna Lumley, Sue Cook, John Craven, Andi Peters, Gaby Roslin, Natasha Kaplinsky, and, of course, Fearne, who again was simply thrilled to be taking part despite the sting in the tail when it was revealed that Wogan was the only presenter to accept money for fronting the BBC's charity appeal. Bands, comedians and celebrity guests waived their appearance fees, as had Fearne. But according to the papers, Wogan received a little over £9,000 for hosting the big night in 2005.

Other presenters and celebrities were taken aback by the revelation. One-time *Children In Need* host, ex-Bucks Fizz singer Cheryl Baker said: 'I am very surprised to hear he takes money for presenting and I think a lot of his fans will be. He has done amazing work for charity. He is a bit of a fool to have taken this money. You would think someone in his position wouldn't need it.'

Wogan, however, who hosted *Children In Need* for 26 years at that time, admitted to being paid but he was also quick to point out that he would gladly do it for free: 'I've never asked for a fee and would happily do it for nothing.' This was reinforced by a Corporation spokesperson: 'It's the BBC who pay Terry, not *Children In Need*. He is not taking any money from the charity. We are not ashamed to pay him and see no reason why it should not continue. If it wasn't for him, *Children In Need* would not be what it is. When Sir Terry presented it originally, it was decided to pay him what is, compared with the commercial cost of a presenter like him, a nominal fee. The fee has continued since and has never been negotiated. We regard it as an honorarium to Sir Terry.'

But Comic Relief didn't agree. As far as they are

concerned, none of the presenters are paid. A spokesperson revealed, 'Neither are the judges or celebrities for *Comic Relief Does Fame Academy*. We feel it's important. We've been terribly fortunate over the years that the people who work with us, including Jonathan Ross, do it for free. Comic Relief's policy is not to pay people. Everything that is done for Comic Relief is done on goodwill.'

Although Fearne had nothing to say on the subject, she appeared neutral. But, as some journalists noted, she always seems very level-headed and responsible about such issues and to spend a great deal more time than many stars twice her age working to raise awareness of cancer and children less fortunate than she was in her own childhood.

One of those occasions was when the parents of Lauren Chambers, a young girl who had a long battle against cancer before her untimely death in spring 2007, got in touch: 'Lauren is someone I feel extremely lucky to have known, even though I only met her at the end of her life. Her parents wrote to me when Lauren was suffering from cancer. They'd asked her to list things she wanted to do and people to meet, and I'm very honoured to have been on that list. I met her just before Christmas [in 2006]. She was critically ill, very thin and couldn't eat much. I visited her a few more times, then in March she passed away.

On stage at the Concert
for Diana, Wembley
Stadium, July 2007.
Fearne describes the
day she interviewed
Prince Harry and Prince
William for this event
as 'the most incredible
experience ever'.

Fearne the style icon. Pictured here on the red carpet of the 2004 MOBO awards in a customised rock-chic outfit (*above left*); at the 2005 National Television Awards in a beautiful black chiffon number (*above right*); at the *Glamour* Women of the Year Awards in a stunning red cocktail dress (*below left*); and at the launch of Lily Allen's 'Lily Loves' collection at New Look (*below right*).

© *REX Features*, © *PA Photos*

An ardent supporter of Comic Relief, alongside stars such as Davina McCall, Russell Brand, Girls Aloud and Gary Lineker, Fearne Cotton was involved in many aspects of 2007's appeal.

© *REX Features*

Loved up.

Fearne and Holly Willoughby, her best friend and fellow presenter, are pretty much inseparable. They are seen here on *Ant and Dec's Saturday Night Takeaway* (*above* and *below right*) and in a promotional shot for *Holly and Fearne Go Dating* (*below left*).

© *REX Features*

Fearne joins *The X-Factor* team:

Above: Fearne, Brian Friedman, Simon Cowell, Dermot O'Leary, Dannii Minogue and Sharon Osbourne (*clockwise from top left*).

Below left: With Dermot O'Leary.

Below right: With 2007 winner Leon Jackson. © *REX Features*

Above left: With *T4* presenter Steve Jones at Topshop's employees' summer party, August 2007.

© *Getty Images*

Above right: With Louis Walsh at the Brits, February 2008.

© *REX Features*

Below left: With Aussie pop princess Kylie Minogue.

© *PA Photos*

Below right: With friend and colleague Reggie Yates.

© *Getty Images*

Fearne Cotton – Britain's brightest young TV star. © *REX Features*

'I was bowled over by what an amazing fighter she was and so strong the whole way through. Whenever we met, she'd have a plan for the day, be it walks or picnics. It was heartbreaking, but I felt honoured to meet her. She made me rethink my reactions to things. Now, if I'm having a whinge about something, I think, "That's pathetic, look at what Lauren went through." As a young girl, you shouldn't have to worry about death, it's so unfair. She taught me to live in the moment, enjoy every day – easy to forget when you're always planning ahead – and cherish friends and family. I have a picture of her on my computer.'

She was also singing the praises of her friend Vikki George, who was one of the founders of the PostPals charity, for which she would eventually become patron in September 2007. It was all about putting a smile on a sick child's face. In fact, it was when Vikki was confined to bed with ME (also known as Chronic Fatigue Syndrome) at the age of sixteen that she found herself feeling bored, frustrated and very much alone and so she decided to help children in a similar position.

Using a Prince's Trust grant, she and two friends set up PostPals, a website which invites people to send 'happy post' to chronically ill children. 'It's been hard work, but definitely worthwhile,' enthuses Vikki. She and fellow ME sufferers Kat Ramsey and Vicky Miles, both of whom are twenty-one, set up the site to put visitors in touch, via secure addresses, with children being treated for genetic conditions or chronic illness.

Site manager Kat, who is from Newquay in Cornwall, was short-listed for the BT ChildLine Awards, which she eventually won. Kat, who was also short-listed for a Whitbread Young Achiever award, was thrilled and remarked: 'I learnt a long time ago that you don't have to be a doctor to save a life.'

Vikki, who is from Little Bookham, a village in Surrey, was diagnosed with ME at the age of ten and eventually forced to leave school when she was just fifteen years old. By the following year her condition had deteriorated so badly that she was virtually unable to move: 'I felt really lonely and cut off from everyone I knew.' When she began to receive post via a ME charity, it made her realise how something as simple as a postcard, email or letter could make a real difference to her day: 'Receiving post became my only contact with the outside world. It gave me a reason to wake up each day.' Knowing this gave Vikki, Kat and Vicky the motivation to set up the site. 'I just wanted other kids to look forward to the thrill of seeing the postman instead of thinking about their illness,' Vikki explained. Because all three young women were bed-bound, a great deal of effort and planning was required to get the project off the ground. 'People with ME have unusual sleep patterns, so we often found ourselves having conference calls and sending emails in the middle of the night,' Vikki continues. The group spent a lot of time researching the project and realised that nothing similar to PostPals existed in the UK. 'It's about two things, really, offering support and revolutionising volunteering,' she continues. 'When people think of helping a child with cancer, they often think it means sponsorship or sending them to Disneyland, but a letter or email – which takes only five minutes and costs the price of a stamp – can also bring a smile and make life more bearable.

'We have people who get in touch from all over the world – Japan, Korea, New Zealand, even Afghanistan.' The site also gives the children a chance to write about themselves and chart their progress. To help visitors understand more about their various conditions, PostPals includes information and links to advice and support groups.

Jon Read says PostPals was very supportive at a time when his nine-year-old son James was undergoing extensive treatment for acute lymphoblastic leukaemia: 'Everybody knows how much kids love getting post but at this time, when James was at an all-time low, it really gave him something to look forward to.'

James's sisters, Philippa and Charlotte, have also received post and now have friends from whom they hear regularly. PostPals believe the brothers and sisters of a sick child also need support because so much time

183

and energy is spent looking after the one who is ill: 'We also want to extend the PostPals scheme for people over the age of eighteen as there is little support available and they often get overlooked.' As Vikki points out, the team is hoping to secure more funding and is busy applying for grants: 'We'd like to do more, like sending children on special trips and, if they pass on, we'd also like to send flowers to their families, but it all adds up. We also send out gift packs, usually art and craft packs, which gives them something to look forward to.' Although PostPals takes up almost all of her time and is often extremely tiring, Vikki says it is very rewarding: 'The difference it makes to people's lives makes it all worthwhile.' And that's why Fearne wanted to use her celebrity status to let everyone know about it.

Chapter 10

The Best Time Ever!

'I wasn't there to dig dirt and be the bad guy; that's not what the BBC wanted. If they'd wanted something more journalistic and hard-hitting they would have got Huw Edwards.'

Three months after flying home from the Oscars ceremony, Fearne headed over to Clarence House, the official home of Prince William and Prince Harry, to film an interview with the royal brothers about the concert they were planning to stage that summer to celebrate the life of their mother, Diana, Princess of Wales, ten years after her tragic death as a result of a bizarre car accident in Paris.

The initial idea for the Concert for Diana was that it should take place at the then all-new Wembley Stadium on 1 July 2007 to tie in with what would have been Diana's 46th birthday, had she lived. As William and Harry explained, they wanted the event to allow people the opportunity to remember their mother with affection by celebrating her achievements rather than the negative aspects of her life that had been growing insistently louder in the press ever since she died. More than anything else they wanted to be fully involved in the organisation of the concert and also with the traditional memorial service set to take place at Guards Chapel, Wellington Barracks, central London, on the tenth anniversary of the day she died, which would be attended by family and relatives as well as friends and representatives from each of her charities.

As William pointed out, 'These events are our way of commemorating our mother's life and so we wanted to make sure they reflected her and her personality as we remember her. When else would you get Kanye West and the English National Ballet on the same bill? But that's our mother all over.'

Their hope, of course, was that the concert would prove to be one of those things that Diana would have adored and approved of. 'This is for her,' elaborated William. 'It's not for any other reason. We want people to remember all the good things she did. After ten years there's been a rumbling of people bringing up the bad and over time people seem to forget all the amazing things she did. This was the best way of bringing that back to life.'

It rankled, for instance, that just two months before the concert, and indeed, while the final preparations were still in progress, that William and Harry were faced with their toughest ordeal yet to protect their mother's memory. That was when they were forced to launch a plea to Channel 4 to remove controversial and graphic images from the documentary scheduled to air three weeks ahead of the concert. In tapes of *Diana: The Witnesses in the Tunnel* doing the media rounds, it was said that the photographs of Diana receiving oxygen and the shots of her inside the car taken immediately after the accident would shock and disgust viewers and would certainly cause great discomfort to William and Harry.

In their defence, Jamie Lowther-Pinkerton, private secretary for the Princes, wrote to Hamish Mykura at Channel 4 to say that William and Harry believed the airing of the photographs would be a gross disrespect to their mother's memory. In his letter he said, 'If it were your or my mother dying in that tunnel, would we want the scene broadcast to the nation? Indeed, would the nation so want it?'

He asked Channel 4 not to broadcast the photographs depicting the crashed car while the Princes' mother lies dying in its wreckage: 'Also, I ask on the Princes' behalf that the shot of the ambulance, with a medic clearly administering emergency treatment to the unseen figure of the Princess, not be broadcast. These photographs, regardless of the fact that they do not actually show the Princess's features, are redolent with the atmosphere and tragedy of the closing moments of her life. As such, they will cause the Princes acute distress if they are shown to a public audience, not just for themselves, but also on their mother's behalf, in the sense of intruding upon the privacy and dignity of her last minutes.' Above all, he concluded, 'the Princes feel that, as her sons, they would be failing in their duty to her now if they did not protect her, as she once did them.'

Channel 4 responded by saying that they had weighed up the concerns of the Princes against the legitimate public interest of the documentary and regardless of this, they were still going to broadcast the images. When the news got out, most of Britain shared the rage that the Princes must have felt, especially as the programme would more or less coincide with William and Harry's concert. On top of that, of course, there was the inevitable avalanche of attention-grabbing books, documentaries and press articles with which they would also have to contend with in the build-up to the anniversary of the crash that killed Diana, her boyfriend Dodi al-Fayed and their chauffeur, Henri Paul, on 31 August 1997.

At the time, Fearne also had her own set of demons to deal with. It seemed objections were being echoed in certain quarters in the BBC at the choice of Fearne to interview William and Harry over and above such respected broadcasters as Huw Edwards and Jeremy Paxman. Apparently some senior BBC journalists were shocked and dismayed; they also claimed the Corporation was treating the interview purely as a piece of showbiz puff rather than a major news story.

'It is an absolute joke that a DJ was allowed to conduct this major interview,' said one unnamed insider. 'Frankly it is ludicrous that a major interview with the sons of the Princess of Wales is not conducted by a proper journalist.' Another insider agreed, and commented, quite cynically, 'I hope she hasn't just asked about who is their favourite singer or who is their favourite band.'

Although the American network NBC was said to be treating the occasion with a more serious undertone and gravity by having veteran broadcaster and news anchor man Matt Lauer interview the Princes, Lauer was also a showbiz presenter, so why all the fuss? Did the BBC or Fearne really have to explain themselves? It seemed they did.

One of the primary reasons for using Fearne was her age and popularity – and of course she proved the right choice for the Princes as well. They would be far more in touch with someone like Fearne than an older broadcaster. Another reason for choosing her was down to the fact that the interview was to be used to plug the live broadcast of the concert. So, the general consensus was that no one would want to sit through a *Panorama* or Martin Bashir-style interview.

As Fearne explained, 'I wasn't there to dig dirt and be the bad guy; that's not what the BBC wanted. If they'd wanted something more journalistic and hard-hitting they would have got Huw Edwards. They wanted something which was going to be compelling and compassionate but still fun.'

When she watched the edited interview back for the first time in a BBC screening room, she was pleased with the result: 'I think they did drop their guard and were very natural. They spoke about their mother for the first time ever, publicly; it was a very special thing to hear.'

They talked, quite emotionally, about missing her: 'It's one of those things that is very sad, but you learn to deal with it and there are plenty of other people out there who have got the same or worse problems than we've had.' They also reminded Fearne and viewers about their mother's charity work, saying, 'She didn't go by what she thought the best thing was to do or be told to do something, she would do it from the heart and fully immerse herself in it and she cared, she cared massively. We were left in no doubt that we were the most important thing in her life, and then after that, there was everyone else, there were all her charities and everything like that, and to us, that's a really good philosophy: she just loved caring for people and she loved helping.'

William and Harry were convinced the event would turn out to be an amazing evening if all went according to plan. In their eyes, this would be the perfect tribute to their music-loving mum. 'She loved exactly the kind of people who are coming,' William continued. 'She loved Sir Elton, George Michael, Michael Jackson, Bryan Adams … We used to catch her dancing to her music but we'd walk out, rather embarrassed. It was a big release for her. It's incredibly exciting: we're thrilled that performers like Rod Stewart, Elton, Bryan Ferry and Status Quo have all agreed to perform. We're also delighted that Andrew Lloyd Webber has created a medley specially for the occasion, which is going to include a few surprise guests, and the English National Ballet, which our mother loved, will also be performing.'

Not only that, but, 'I think combining our mother's tastes with our own favourite acts will make this event truly unique. It's the perfect opportunity to celebrate her life with a concert with people smiling and having fun, waving their arms in the air, like they just don't care!' added Harry.

And to all intents and purposes, that is what they got.

The concert was broadcast in 140 different countries across the world with an estimated potential audience of 500 million homes. Actually, it all started out as far back as the previous December, when over 22,000 tickets went on sale and sold out, quite remarkably, in just 17 minutes. Surely that alone must have convinced everyone that Diana was loved just as much in death as when she was alive?

With 63,000 people turning out to watch the concert and two short intermissions, the event kicked off at 6pm and ran for well over four hours; in the process it raised over £150,000 for each of the eight charities that William and Harry wanted to benefit most. Although the occasion was first and foremost a tribute concert, it was also a stage to raise money. 'Yes,' said Harry, 'that's why we decided that the proceeds from the concert should go to the Diana, Princess of Wales Memorial Fund and those charities that were most closely linked with our mother at the end of her life. In addition to these we are also hoping to donate money to Centrepoint, of which William is now a patron, and Sentebale, which I set up in memory of my mother to help AIDS victims and orphans in Lesotho.'

Although it was difficult for William and Harry to pinpoint which of Diana's charitable achievements and allegiances they are most proud of, it was her work for HIV and AIDS sufferers, as well as those who have been maimed and injured by landmines, that are two areas that still stand out in most people's minds. Of course as her sons, the Princes were immensely proud of everything their mother did to help others and they were hoping, in their own way, to continue some of her work and try to achieve as much as Diana did with some of the charities she had been involved with during her life. One of those charities was Centrepoint.

William remembers well visiting hostels for homeless people with his mother when she was a patron: 'I was so struck then by the importance of the work it does. I want to do what I can to support their staff in helping give homeless people not only shelter, but also advice on how, through Centrepoint's learning and life skills initiatives, they might take their lives forward with new hope and security. It's the general sense of companionship between the staff and young people that always impresses me. I come away completely uplifted myself whenever I visit. I know my mother felt the same.'

Harry was also very proud of the work they were doing in Lesotho, very much inspired by his mother's work with AIDS: 'Since I made the documentary *Prince Harry in Lesotho* in 2004, we have been investing in projects in Lesotho – which we're now doing through Sentebale. And I've recently become patron of WellChild, a charity that supports seriously ill children and their families, and I'm keen to support the carers and volunteers who do such an amazing and challenging job. In fact, we're holding a lunch on the day before the concert at Wembley Stadium as a treat for some of the children, their families and the WellChild staff who help look after them. Hopefully they will be able to see some of the stars rehearsing, and get to see the stadium all set up for the big day!'

As she was about to become the patron of PostPals that September, Fearne was quite naturally keen to hear how William and Harry were trying to encourage youngsters to get involved with charity work. 'I think you'd be amazed at how many children are involved in charity work of some kind or other,' Harry expounded. 'Be it through groups like the Girl Guides or Scouts, taking part in my grandfather's awards scheme or just doing fun things for charity with their school or local community. Great examples of how young people are contributing to society, both in a charitable sense and in starting and running vital initiatives such as anti-bullying programmes in schools, are provided by the Diana Award winners, some of whom will also be joining us for lunch at Wembley.'

It was pretty obvious from watching the finished footage that both William and Harry were delighted to have Fearne asking the questions for the interview they agreed to film for the BBC. Despite what prophets of gloom and doom at the BBC were saying, she had asked the sort of questions that covered exactly what the BBC wanted and so when the interview was broadcast on 29 June, the day before the concert, it achieved exactly the result that she said it would, which was to be, she repeated, 'compelling and compassionate and fun'.

She was also thrilled for another reason: 'Getting to interview the chaps was the most incredible experience ever. They are the two most polite, down-to-earth funny boys ever. I could have chatted to them all day. I'm hoping to catch up with them again on the big day, fingers crossed. It's all in my master plan to become their new common best mate.'

Not that she really needed any such plans. Her stunning good looks, fun-loving nature and adorable charm were enough to do just that. In fact, it wasn't long after the interview had been shown and the concert played that rumours started to circulate that William had indeed taken a firm fancy to Fearne. At the time, he had recently broken up with girlfriend Kate Middleton and reportedly revealed his true feelings to Fearne.

But according to Fearne, she wasn't really interested. She may have been, she said, had she been single, and then, yes, maybe it would have been fun to pursue. Of course, William wasn't the first interviewee to be smitten. R&B star Usher declared her to be 'completely gorgeous' and, as we have already discovered, Robbie

Williams proposed marriage live on camera, but, 'There was no way that I'd marry Robbie. Apart from anything else, I could never be part of that celebrity world.'

As for William, Fearne says, 'In person I found him very suave and sophisticated, a proper gent in all ways. But even if romance had bloomed between us, I can't imagine that the Palace would have encouraged it. I'm far too common. Having said that, I think I'd make a really good queen. I wear a tiara well; I could change the National Anthem to Led Zep's "Good Times Bad Times". And I'd issue a decree that every home in Britain must have a record player and a decent collection of vinyl.'

When she told her parents what had happened, they thought it was hilarious. In an interview with the *Daily Star*, Fearne's father, Mick Cotton, was extremely proud: 'We still can't believe it. Prince William is smitten with our daughter! She'd definitely make a fantastic queen. We knew she was interviewing William and his brother Harry for the Diana Memorial Concert but we never dreamed something like this would happen. They got on really well and we're chuffed to bits that he took a shine to her.'

But then again, Fearne has been constantly fascinated by the royal family and says that she has always been interested in the work the Princess did for charity, even though she would have only been fifteen years old when

Diana died. And as if to prove the point, she had already become involved with Comic Relief six years earlier when she and Chris Parker visited Kenya, and to this day she still exchanges letters with a young woman she met out there.

She had also, of course, presented the Live 8 concert in Hyde Park in 2005 in support of the aims of the 'Make Poverty History' campaign, which hoped to help put pressure on world leaders to drop the debt of the world's poorest nations, increase and improve aid, and negotiate Fair Trade rules in the interests of poorer countries. In addition, she was named youth ambassador for Macmillan Cancer in the year that followed.

She was so very grateful to the Macmillan nurses, who looked after her nan when she was ill. 'They were amazing,' she said. 'I'd worked with them on their annual World's Biggest Coffee Morning, and then they asked me if I'd be an ambassador. I couldn't believe it, it's an absolute honour.'

She knew only too well how hard it can be to talk to friends about things like cancer: 'When my nan was diagnosed, I found it hard to deal with and was unsure if anyone else would understand.' She didn't want others to suffer alone in silence, as she perhaps had done, and that was the idea behind fronting the then new Macmillan Youthline. It was launched to help youngsters from the ages of twelve to twenty-one who needed someone to talk to, which of course made Fearne the ideal choice.

As for the Diana Concert itself, this was an incredible day, raved Fearne. According to the blog she posted on her MySpace: 'William and Harry worked so hard and put on one hell of a show. It was a gorgeous day with an indescribable atmosphere. I had so much fun interviewing people backstage, such as P. Diddy, who I never knew was a huge Princess Diana fan, Pharrell Williams, who I thought was a bit moody, and Dennis Hopper, who wins the award for best suit of the day!

'So, I had been interviewing people for a good few hours and decided it was time for a loo break. I walked across the Green Room where all the celebs were hanging out, passed Beckham and his bleached hair, Kanye West and his thirty bodyguards and found the little loo in the corner of the room. The lock said empty, so in I walk, but it turned out someone was in there. I had just exposed that someone to the whole room of celebs. And he was on the phone, having a wee with his twinkle out. And that someone was Kiefer Sutherland! How embarrassing! I frantically apologised and slammed the door. He eventually came back out where I apologised some more. He was very, very sweet and said it wasn't a problem and then said he would hold the door for me while I went to the loo as there was no lock. What a gent. So Mr 24 stood there and guarded the door.'

But, according to *Now* magazine, Fearne – who had gone bright red with embarrassment – said she knew she couldn't run off because she might have had to interview him later and, 'I wouldn't just be able to say, "Nice to meet you, even though I've already met you and your willy." I was so flustered, though, that I couldn't wee.'

No sooner had she finished her work interviewing the stars backstage at the Diana Concert than Fearne returned to continue filming the new ITV1 dating show that she was making with Holly Willoughby, which had been in production since late May. The two women have been best mates ever since their days on CBBC and, as mentioned before, they would often spend time together when they weren't working. Even if they did have harmless fun most of the time, there were occasions when things got a little out of control. But, according to Fearne, 'We used to have a laugh, though. We went to America a few years ago and made friends with a random group of lads. We're still friends with them now. We'd go out in the afternoon and not get back until the next day; it was so raucous. I have some amazing photos from that holiday that have never been seen.'

Holly agrees: 'Fearne has a picture of me looking absolutely wasted. I've got a drink in one hand and my eyes are rolling to the back of my head. In fact, it's not just a picture: it's a huge A3 size painting, which is hanging up in Fearne's spare bedroom. We're both quite tactile people and flirt all the time, but I've never had a guy come up to me; I've always had to do the chasing – I must be totally unapproachable.'

Things are much the same for Fearne: 'I've asked out every guy that I've ever been on a date with. I don't know if boys think it's a cliché or are scared, but they don't make the move. There's none of that: "Would you like to go out for a drink?" We need more of that.'

Like the day when she was Holly's bridesmaid at her wedding to television producer Dan Baldwin at Amberley Castle in west Sussex in August 2007. 'We used to go there for Mother's Day and special days when we were kids,' says Holly. 'From a child, I knew that's where I'd get married. The day was amazing. When the vicar said, "You are now husband and wife, you may kiss the bride," you say: "Oh my God, we're married!" I'd fantasised about being married since I was a little girl and dressed up in my mum's wedding dress.'

Decked out in a white dress with a black sash, Fearne joined Sarah Cawood and another eight bridesmaids in the midst of a host of celebrities that included Dermot O'Leary, Nicole Appleton and Tamzin Outhwaite among the 150 guests. As one guest summed up, 'It was an amazing day. Holly couldn't stop smiling and everything went to plan.'

It was also telling of their friendship with each other (and with their peers) when they collected the Best Entertainment Presenter award at the National Television Awards at London's Royal Albert Hall on 31 October 2007 on behalf of Ant and Dec, who were unable to attend because they were in Australia busy filming *I'm A Celebrity … Get Me Out of Here!*.

Proving something of a phenomenon in television circles, Ant and Dec have been racking up TV hit after TV hit. Coincidentally, in one episode of *Ant and Dec's Saturday Night Takeaway,* their most recent show, Holly and Fearne are seen together again – this time 'beating the boys' by 20 seconds as they bounced around an assault course in a beach buggy. The pair were seen jumping up and down with joy that they had managed to pull it off. Introduced into the sixth series of the programme, the 'beat the boys' feature shows Ant and Dec challenging two celebrities each week to try and beat them around an assault course using specially modified vehicles.

In many ways, Ant and Dec's show was a bit like *I'm A Celebrity …* only when *Celebrity* started out, it was probably with generally low expectations until Katie Price, then known as Jordan, Peter Andre and Kerry Katona took part and turned the show into one of the most popular and gripping programmes around. Once again, Ant and Dec presided to see that the group of celebrities dumped in a remote part of the Australian jungle were properly deprived of food before they were made to undergo challenging – and often horrible – ordeals to win some provisions for their camp.

The longer they suffered, the more food they got. Following in the format of so many other reality shows, back in the UK the viewers were able to vote on which celebrity had to endure which trial and it was also the viewers who voted the contestants off. The idea was simple but proved incredibly popular television, in much the same way as *Ant and Dec's Saturday Night Takeaway*.

Long before all of that, of course, Fearne had seen in the New Year with a 1950s fancy dress party for friends at her home in south-west London, which she describes as debauched and chaotic: 'People got wasted like they were off their heads on cheap vodka in the park after school. Loo seats were ripped from their homes, light fixtures smashed, people rolling around in the street, pink ladies trying to climb my chimney in my lounge, and one guy even locked himself in his car and then repeatedly set the alarm off until 5am!'

Equally chaotic, in many ways, was how Holly spent six years getting gunged every Saturday morning from the age of seventeen (a popular feature of Saturday morning TV when the presenter or guest or both would get covered in gunge), but today her career is almost as bright as Fearne's; it has been, in fact, ever since she took over *Streetmate* from Davina McCall on ITV2, and before she was spotted by Storm (the same modelling agency who discovered Kate Moss) when she was fourteen, became the face of Rimmel, the body of Pretty Polly and appeared on covers of countless women's magazines, picked up some guest presenting gigs on *CD:UK* and *Dancing On Ice*, won a BAFTA for Best Presenter and was a regular presenter on *Ministry Of Mayhem*, where she first met husband-to-be, Dan Baldwin.

But unlike Fearne, Holly was one of a group of presenters in children's television who were said to drink until 5am. It was, she says, 'like being at college, except with money. We didn't feel like grown-ups as we were just being so wild and naughty. There's very little pressure in kids' TV. No one's on your case, and if you mess up, no one cares. There's a lot that would shock people about kids' TV. One day someone will blow the lid off it.' But for now, she was keeping quiet. Well, sort of …

'I remember when we filmed *Ministry Of Mayhem* in Maidstone, the guests had to stay with us overnight and it was like being on tour. We'd all be put up in this hotel with the celebrity guests, so, of course, it went bonkers. You just knew you were in for a wild time the night before. All the boy bands were great. Girls Aloud were always crazy, too.'

On top of that, she continues, 'I spent three years of

my life dressed as a French maid. I wore the outfit on *Ministry Of Mayhem*, and it certainly got a response, but I don't like to think about all the boys who harboured crushes on me. I inevitably ended up covered in cake when I wore it, and cream is just the worst thing. No matter how hard you scrub in the shower, you can't get the smell of a custard pie off your skin.'

She also remembers, 'There were times when we went straight from the hotel bar to going live on air at 6am. It doesn't help when you read the script and find you've got to drink anchovies in custard with some eight-year-old! That day I was sick live on TV.'

But that proved to be the least of her concerns. When she attended a friend's wedding, it turned out that everyone at her school had already been hounded by a journalist trying to dig up some dirt on her: 'He got hold of them through Friends Reunited and was offering them crazy money, but not one of them could find anything. It's not because they didn't want to; I'm just too much of a sad case. The only time I ever got in trouble was when I threw my shoe across the classroom. Hardly sex, drugs and rock'n'roll.'

If anything, Holly is one of the few celebrities who won't object to the paparazzi. And she has good reason: 'They've never caused me any trouble – if they want a photo, I give them a photo. One of them even did me a huge favour. I was late getting to the BAFTAs and there was a Tube strike, so I couldn't get a cab anywhere. This pap was taking photos of me looking all frantic and worried, so I asked him if he'd drive me to the awards. We were driving and I just said, "Well, this is weird, isn't it?" But I won, so I always feel slightly indebted to them.'

All the same, she and Fearne have been inseparable since the day they met. Perhaps that's why working together on *Holly and Fearne Go Dating* was so appealing. 'The idea of the show, six in all,' explained Holly, 'was to find a single person, somebody looking for love, and spend time with them and see what makes them tick, what they think they want in a partner … We then set out to find them two dates: one my choice and one Fearne's.'

But there was more to it than that, as Fearne continued: 'When the date happens, time is spent with both potential partners and at the end of the night we wait, nervously, to see if there's any chance of romance! We also see who has chosen the best potential partner. I, of course, want to beat Holly desperately! And like Holly, I have always loved the idea that I could set two people up who would really hit it off and make a great couple.'

When the first show appeared on the screens that September, rather than give the programme a critical review, journalist Rin Simpson, writing in the *Western Mail*, preferred to examine whether anyone can plan love or if it was all simply a matter of chance. Indeed, could Holly and Fearne's idea work if they were setting out to meet one of love's losers; to get to know their subject, to listen to stories of dating disasters, find out the sort of places where they've met previous lovers and build a picture of what's been going on, what's going wrong and what sort of person they might be compatible with? The contestant then gets to choose who they think could be Mr or Mrs Right from the two dates set up by Holly and Fearne.

'It sounds slightly more organised and thought-out than the random happening of, say, meeting a stranger at a nightclub or bus stop,' praised Ingrid Collins, a consultant psychologist at London's Medical Centre in Harley Street, who specialises in love and relationships. 'But you can't necessarily tell who will make a great couple. There is always the wildcard element, that magic spark – or lack of it – that is the mystery ingredient.'

On paper, Collins continued, 'Two people might seem absolutely made for each other, but in reality can leave each other cold or go for each other's throats! There are dozens of elements that need to come together for a relationship to bloom in any circumstance, let alone the pressurised atmosphere of a situation engineered specifically to create a new couple.'

And of course she was right. 'On a conscious level,' she explained, 'all the usual rules apply. Is the person pleasant, stimulating or exciting to be with? Do they find each other sexually alluring? Does a talkative person find a good listener? Does a shy person find an extrovert? Does their behaviour and dress style give appropriate messages that will be accepted by the person's peer group? There are hundreds of variations on these themes.'

But no one could answer that, simply because you can't predict love and, of course, if you could, there'd be a lot less heartache in the world. Making matters worse, perhaps, was the fact that the dating game has turned into such a multi-million-pound industry and so perhaps finding the right partner is now more difficult than ever before.

Although Internet dating agencies in the UK have an estimated six million subscribers and *DatingDirect*, Britain's biggest online dating firm, was sold for more than £27 million in January 2007, the industry continues to grow. Speed-dating events are held in bars, hotels, restaurants, even on trains. And you can go on a 'date in the dark', a 'love cruise' or a 'singles holiday'. Of course there's also the ever-faithful blind date, arranged by a caring (or interfering) friend or relative. Scientific it isn't, but love isn't something that can really be pinned down, analysed and made to work, no matter how much we try; not even on television.

Even so, online reviewer Andy Williams shared the

general consensus of other critics that the show was a 'mish-mash of half-baked ideas, as illustrated by the bizarre title sequence in which giant versions of our two matchmakers stride through a futuristic city doing their make-up while a reworked "Sowing the Seeds of Love" plays in the background. We're introduced to the duo as they're chatting in a sports car while driving to their first singleton, Charlotte, a gardening expert with a penchant for 1950s clothing and art. After a brief chat they discover the girl and her mother share a special bond and are never apart. She lives in a remote village and rarely goes out with people her own age.

'Not only that,' continued Williams, but, 'Holly and Fearne aren't very convincing in their roles. They constantly talk over each other and seem more like they were thrown together by the production company, given they clearly have nothing in common. This is demonstrated perfectly in their choice of venues to look for prospective men. Holly decides to travel to an urban poetry club, while Fearne heads to an environmental festival as she's decided Charlotte needs a "green person".

'Holly's choice of location is described as "one of the coolest nights out in Bristol", a recipe for success if I've ever heard it. The pair wander round, taking Polaroids of random men, and interviewing a select few who catch their eye. They narrow it down to a creative writer who also has a passion for 1950s clothing and Simon, a dull man whose claim to fame is that he used to be a butler to the Queen. Of course Holly incorrectly chooses the latter to have a dinner date with Charlotte.

'The day after, Fearne heads to the festival where she uncovers one of the most idiotic people to ever grace this earth. Ben is your archetypal "wacky" guy – he wears "crazy" clothes and thinks all his own jokes are hilarious. "Of course, I'm single," he claims, "I'm always single." Surely the alarm bells should have rung, but no, Fearne thinks he would be perfect for timid Charlotte and picks him for dinner at Hell's Kitchen.'

Williams concludes by adding, 'There is such a lack of concern for anything in the show, and the only emotion is when we learn who's won this episode. It turned out to be Holly, even though Charlotte said, "There was no spark" between her and Simon. She obviously chose him just to get away from the unbearable Ben. And that's where we left it. There was no follow-up about what she learnt, or if she'll make changes to her life. Just Charlotte stood outside the restaurant, alone, saying that Simon probably "never wanted to see me ever again".'

As Williams observed, it did make one wonder if the whole show was just another excuse for ITV1 to try something supposedly exciting that didn't quite deliver its promise. And perhaps making matters worse was the fact that somehow the basics for *Holly and Fearne Go Dating* were way off course.

Despite what many critics were saying, and perhaps what gave the show some kind of hope and saving grace, was the fact that the girls did appear to enjoy playing Cupid even if they weren't, in some people's eyes, particularly good at it. As Holly points out, 'I have always liked setting people up and take great delight in getting that tingling feeling that two people might just be great together. I think it's no secret that I am a complete romantic. My thinking is: "How will you ever find your prince if you don't start kissing some frogs?" Just get on with it! Whereas I think that Fearne's approach is more direct and a little bit more cheeky.'

Fearne agrees: 'I'd definitely say that I'm more mischievous in my matchmaking skills but that makes it all the more fun and that's why I think we complement each other.' She did much the same off-camera as well: 'I set up one of my boy mates with one of my friend's mates and now they have a baby together and I'm godmother! I'm very proud of that one.'

It also helped that both girls have had their fair share of bad experiences with dating. Fearne remembers when she went on 'a really awful blind date where the guy I was with snogged another girl in the club we were in and I caught him out'. And on another occasion, she was even more mortified when a guy she met on a plane arrived for their dinner date wearing a full-blown cowboy outfit; she didn't know where to look. She told

Heat magazine: 'This hot American bloke sat next to me on a plane to Miami and we were chatting away throughout the flight. He said he was coming to London in three weeks, so we arranged to meet up. I walked into this restaurant and he was in full-blown cowboy outfit. It was terrible, and I just had to sit there!'

But then again, she does seem to have caught the nation by storm, especially as far as guys are concerned. According to *More* magazine, 'If you're male, 25, live with your parents, drive a Ford Fiesta and sex lasts for 22 minutes, congratulations, you're average.' This fact was taken from a survey of 2,000 young women, who revealed that the average guy watches television for 24 hours a week, lusts after Fearne in his M&S undies, beneath regular-cut denims and a stripy T-shirt. He does not smoke and is not a big boozer. Hard-working, he earns over £26,000 a year, has been to university and is unlikely to get married much before he is thirty.

Holly, on the other hand, is perhaps not so high on the list of celebrities that most guys would like to sleep with. But like Fearne, she too has some bad dating moments. Although one tabloid said her worst nightmare was when a taco hit her in the face, according to one of Fearne's blogs on her MySpace that is what happened to her, not Holly: 'I went to a small Mexican restaurant with my boyfriend. I sat down opposite a couple eating while my boyfriend went to pick up some napkins. The next thing I know the lady opposite stood up and threw her whole plate of tacos at her fella. The thing is, she missed him and hit me straight in the face. There I was, covered in beans, cheese, sauce, the lot! They both stormed out and I was left covered in shit with everyone looking at me! They hadn't raised their voices at all prior to this, so a total surprise attack!' Although she wasn't laughing at the time, it appears she was when she recounted the tale.

In the end, though, both girls agreed that 'if there were a wedding to come out of our television matchmaking, it would be one of the happiest moments of our lives!' And as that hadn't happened on the first series of their dating programme, Fearne decided to introduce a dating spin-off segment on to *The Xtra Factor* that she had been hosting for ITV2 since earlier in the year. Interestingly enough, her first attempt for matchmaking was to set up Dannii Minogue …

Chapter 11

And In the End ...

'I once went on **Big Brother's Little Brother** *without even having seen* **Big Brother** *because I just wanted to go and hang out with him.'*

It was December 2007, a few weeks before Christmas, when Fearne returned home from her travels to India, where she had witnessed the work being done in Chennai by World Vision and their Street Children Project. Her trip had given her the chance to see for herself, first-hand, what was being done out there and the difference it was already making, as well as providing her with an insight into what still needed to be tackled. She met with World Vision staff, street families, runaway children, teachers and volunteers. And she also got to know some incredibly strong and courageous people and learnt so much about their stories of grief and hope.

She had kept a diary, recording the sights and sounds of the places she visited and the astounding stories she had been told, as well as collecting together her own thoughts and reflections from her one-week stay. The idea was to share this exclusively online with the World Vision website during the 24 Hour Famine campaign in March 2008, for which she was the official ambassador. 'It's such an easy thing for kids to get involved in,' she enthuses. 'And it's a good way to demonstrate exactly what that hunger feels like. I actually didn't take part in a famine when I was at school because my mum was a bit nervous about the idea, but it is safe and it doesn't matter if you can't do the whole twenty-four hours. It is really, really hard to go without food.'

In one extract that she had already given to the charity to use as a taste of what was upcoming, she spoke of her journey through the busy streets of Chennai: 'There are cars, motorbikes and people everywhere. Every time you look out the car window there is something to see. So many colours, smells and noises simultaneously. There's a weird contrast of people rushing to get to work, shopkeepers going about their daily business and children running to school, mixed with women sitting on the side of the road with their babies and children, begging in ragged clothes. It's hard at times to take it all in as there is so much around you.'

And when she spoke about her new role as ambassador, she sounded thrilled: 'I am really excited to be fronting this year's campaign. I've been sponsoring a child through World Vision for the last few years and know what an important and vital job they do. We're asking for help to get kids in Chennai off the streets and instead give them the opportunity of a better, safer life and future.'

It was something she felt most strongly about. Now in its 22nd year, the 24 Hour Famine was the biggest youth fundraising event in Britain, which had seen over two million people helping to raise over £20 million for projects around the world and allowed World Vision to continue its ongoing commitment to partner with developing communities in nearly a hundred countries as they worked to improve and transform the lives of millions of people living in poverty.

The 2008 campaign was promising to encourage young people across the UK to be sponsored to go without something important to them for one day so that others wouldn't have to. Funds raised would help to make a life-changing difference to street children in Chennai, India, who live in danger of abuse and exploitation and go without many of life's basics such as clean safe water, shelter or regular nutritious meals.

By working with community organisations in Chennai, World Vision's aim is to help improve the lives of thousands of street and working children in the city by providing them with safe places to live, while running initiatives such as children's clubs, giving them an education and workshops to learn a trade, counselling and rehabilitation programmes, which in turn would help many children living and working on the street to live a new life in a safe environment, with access to essential services and better prospects for their future.

Feeling slightly shattered from her trip, with a fuzzy head and somewhat disorientated, Fearne was relaxing at home the day she got back and feeling very thankful about the simplest of things: 'I am listening to Adele's "Hometown Glory", have just eaten me tea and am about to have a hot choc. It's weird being back and I have the most wonderful, strange and sad memories of India.'

Some of those memories, she had decided to share with her 60,000 MySpace friends by updating her blog on the same day that she returned home. Having never been to India before, she said she had set off with an open mind, open heart and very open eyes: 'When we landed it was around 5am but when I walked out of the airport the only reason I knew it was night was the fact that the sky was dark – apart from that it could have been day time: people milling about, children running in the road, cars honking their horns ... It was all go.'

The next morning, she continues, 'My first daylight impression of Chennai wasn't much different; just slightly busier, if possible. People everywhere ... Cars pulling out of every turning, horns beeping every second, cows walking about, little shops and stalls selling everything going. It just all seemed so chaotic and alive. The first place I visited was a small church where street kids are being housed. There are around 40,000 street kids in Chennai alone each year! Only about 12 kids can stay at this church through World Vision at the moment but we are hoping to raise funds for a new centre where 2,000 kids can stay until either their families are found again or a new home can be arranged for these kids.'

When she arrived, she met two children who were brother and sister. The girl was eight and the boy aged around three: 'They had been found on the street the week before with no parents, no clothes and no food. Their father had passed away and their mother was mentally ill so World Vision had taken them in, clothed and fed them. They seemed calm and happy, playing with their new pens and paper. They were such strong little kids. The sister had become a mother figure to her brother already and seemed to do this with ease. To me the whole thing seemed so crazy. These little kids weren't crying and screaming because their mum wasn't there; they had clicked in to survivor mode and were just getting on with it.'

She also visited lots of families who lived in communities on the street. One street had about 12 families dotted about along the pavement: 'Since the monsoon season World Vision have managed to provide a plastic cover for each family to create some shelter for them, but apart from this, they literally just have a few pots and rugs. One young girl of eighteen invited me to her "house". I met her mother who also told me she had two sons, all of them living under this plastic shelter and on about fifty pence a day from her cleaning job in a nearby house. The eighteen-year-old, Sangrita, was studying as World Vision had managed to provide her with books and school equipment, but her mother wants her to stop and start working so the family can earn more money.

'Many families are faced with this: the parents are reluctant to let the children go to school as they will earn less money. World Vision are trying to teach the adults that in the long-term they will benefit from their children having some skills and are helping as many kids into school as possible. We visited the main train station too, as around four to eight kids a day arrive in Chennai, believing they will find work, opportunities and adventure! They travel from all over India and end up living on the streets like so many others. We went to try and spot lonesome children getting off the train as the World Vision workers do every day. They take the children to their offices for counselling to see if they can return home and find out why they have run away, and if they have nowhere to go, the next step is to give them shelter, food and education for as long as possible. This is why the new centre is so desperately needed.'

Although she said she had literally a million other stories to share about the people she met – 'like the woman I met at the station who had arrived three days before and given birth. There she stood with her two-day-old baby, so thin she could barely hold him up. She had come back feeling very lucky to have met all these people and to have seen so many places: 'India is a beautiful country but parts like Chennai need a lot of help right now. I won't forget any of the faces I have met, stories I have heard, the sweet smells of India, the kids I did colouring in with at the pre-school, who laughed and laughed, the madness of the roads ... It was all so mad, but such a great experience.'

Aside from being home and getting ready for Christmas, she also had the semi-final of *The X Factor* to think about the day after she returned. And it was pretty clear who her favourites were: she really liked Leon Jackson because 'he gets really nervous and I like that you get to see his vulnerability. I think Rhydian is great, too. Careerwise he could be really successful. He brings something so magnificent to the stage, and at this point I would put my money on him' – which just goes to show how wrong she could sometimes be: it was Jackson who walked away the winner, ten days before Christmas.

But in her opinion none of the contestants could compare to the previous year's winner, Leona Lewis: 'I love Leona – I mean, to me she explains why *X Factor* exists. She was a true talent that was found from nowhere and I think *X Factor* this year is going to find it very difficult to find someone up to her standard. I think this year the competition's different in that it's more entertaining but I think she's just the most amazing singer and she came on the show the other week and I couldn't believe how great she was. She was amazing.'

She also adored Dermot O'Leary: 'I bloody love the boy! I once went on *Big Brother's Little Brother* without even having seen *Big Brother* because I just wanted to go and hang out with him. He asked me a load of questions and I literally blagged the whole thing because I didn't know what I was talking about. He's given *The X Factor* his own touch – he's perfect for it.' And she admits how well she got along with him during the production of the show: 'We have a special *X Factor* handshake we do when we see each other which is way geeky, but I love it.' But she had no plans to keep the judges in line on *The Xtra Factor* sofa. Oh no, she said, those are 'my favourite bits when they all argue and disagree so I will be positively encouraging it'.

Although many, like Fearne, thought Rhydian was a sure-fire winner, others considered that perhaps it was Kylie Minogue's duet of her own 1990 hit 'Better The Devil You Know' with Jackson that swung the final vote, although there were some who wondered if Kylie's outfit, described by many as nothing more than a body stocking, was entirely suitable for a family talent show or indeed appropriate for her duet.

Interestingly enough, the video for Kylie's original hit also met with friction. Not from the press but from her then record label, Pete Waterman's PWL. As far as he was concerned it was light years away from the image that he wanted to project for his prize star. Compared to the more innocent videos that preceded it, Waterman thought that having a video that featured a revealingly dressed, perfectly toned Kylie, dancing madly and snuggling herself up into the arms of a naked black man twice her size, would send out shockwaves both to her fans and the media. But he needn't have worried. If anything, it made the press sit up and take notice, as well as giving Kylie the serious street cred she had up until that time so craved. Not that it mattered to Jackson, who was just thrilled that Dannii had persuaded her sister to help him out on his big night.

Series 4 of *The X Factor* started its new run in August, and several months before that the show's infamously harsh judges had been searching for the nation's next big pop singer. Simon Cowell, Sharon Osbourne, Louis Walsh and the then new additional judge, Kylie's younger sister, Dannii Minogue, had been holding open auditions across the country and they had, it was said, directed their acerbic put-downs to an unprecedented 150,000 acts, from the tuneful to the talentless.

'We've had a reformed lap dancer, a woman who did impressions of a horse and two lads who performed their own song called "Burger Flipper",' said Simon, who was also responsible for creating such other talent shows as *Pop Idol*, *Britain's Got Talent*, *America's Got Talent* and *American Idol*. As usual, the chosen acts were put into categories: Boys 14–24, Girls 14–24, 25 and Over, and Groups. The judges are then assigned a category and compete against each other as they train their acts for success in the live heats, which eventually go to a public vote.

The act with that indefinable 'X Factor' would scoop a £1 million recording contract, just like the previous winners, Shayne Ward and Leona Lewis. And going on previous years, the first single of every winner went straight in at Number One. Dermot O'Leary was recruited to take over from Kate Thornton as the new host of the main show, while Fearne replaced Ben

Shephard for *The Xtra Factor*, the spin-off show that took viewers behind the scenes.

One of the new features that she introduced to the programme was 'Cotton Buddies', a kind of dating section in which Fearne played matchmaker to fix up lonely auditionees:'I realised a lot of the people who are sitting in the holding area waiting to audition are single and bored. So I wander around and try and set people up while they wait. It's fun and takes their minds off being nervous.' In many ways, it sounded as if this was to get her own back on pals such as Davina McCall. When Fearne was single, she was constantly trying to set her up on dates:'I absolutely adore Davina, she's the loveliest lady ever. But she's always trying to set me up with her friends, but I'm terrible with guys – I just hang around hoping they come over and chat to me.'

She remembers one occasion in particular when she was snubbed while she was at a concert and asked for a guy's phone number: 'You can't worry about being knocked back. I got turned down: I met this guy at a gig and thought he was lovely. I got chatting to him and found out he didn't have a girlfriend so I asked for his number but he knocked me back.' Rather than be deterred from approaching men in the future, she said, 'You just have to go on to the next one.'

She also presented a Christmas Special of the best and worst auditions during the series that looked back at some of the highs and the lows, including the first auditions of finalists Alisha Bennett, Same Difference and Andy Williams. Representing the worst auditions was the lady who opened the series: fifty-five-year-old Susan Perkins from Kent, who had hoped to walk back through the doors as a superstar, and Kick-off Kelly, who before her big moment boldly claimed that she didn't just have the X Factor, but also the 'Wow Factor' as well!

Another contender was Toshiko, the Japanese woman who travelled almost 6,000 miles to the Birmingham auditions just to meet Simon and tell him how much she liked him, and how It's About Time, a singing quartet consisting of two sisters and their husbands, were reduced to tears. After cutting the group off mid-song, Simon gave them the advice they didn't want to hear: that they were better off carol singing at Christmas to make themselves a bit of money and that, he concluded, was about 'as far as it will ever go'.

The judges also revealed their favourite audition moments. Sharon and Louis reflected on the best of the worst, while Simon revealed that his favourite-ever audition was Same Difference – one of his final acts.

But probably the highlight of *The Xtra Factor* itself was when Fearne set up Dannii on a champagne lunch date with an auditionee. His name was Chris Gale and he was a forty-five-year-old marketing director. They shared a picnic on the lawns outside the NEC Birmingham until

Louis Walsh, who needed Dannii back inside for the auditions (one of which was Chris's own), interrupted them. Things got worse when Chris sang Neil Diamond's 'Hello Again' and Danni didn't put him through to the next round. He was devastated: 'Dannii, you can't say no. Did you not feel me singing this to you? Surely it's about passion, isn't it?'

Later, outside the audition, he told Fearne that Dannii was playing hard to get: 'Maybe she's done that because she just wants to separate our new wonderful relationship from the whole *X Factor* thing.' But it seemed that that was just wishful thinking on Chris's part. Back in the audition hall, Dannii buried her head in her hands after he left and Simon, unaware of their earlier meeting, told her: 'That was like you just dumped him!'

Dannii, of course, was still being thought of as the girl next door who has spent a lifetime living in the shadow of her more famous sister. But now, perhaps, she was about to get her moment due to her new lease of life as the most popular of *The X Factor* judges and an array of album and single releases, including reissues of her 1997 and 2003 albums *Girl*, *Neon Nights* and *Unleashed*, as well as singles such as 'Touch Me Like That' and the digital album *Club Disco*, which peaked at Number Two on the UK Dance Album chart. These threatened to send her popularity through the roof and even overtake the success of Kylie.

Most seem fascinated by the way Dannii has weathered the storm of always being compared to Kylie and how she has struggled to find respect from the critics, who, more often than not, have portrayed her as nothing more than a 'wannabe'. But she was a child star long before Kylie, acting in such Australian soaps as *Skyways* and *The Sullivans* before her sister followed suit, and as a teen in *Home and Away*, where she found fame as punk Emma, and then, by reinventing herself in a similar way to her sister later on, she found stardom as a singer. During this time she would notch up nineteen Top 20 hits and have four top-selling albums over sixteen years that have earned her a string of awards and nominations.

Interestingly enough, she has always seemed to play second to Kylie, but let's not forget that Dannii was the first Minogue sister to be internationally regarded as a gay icon and to play multiple performances at the *Sydney Gay and Lesbian Mardi Gras* and at the G-A-Y nightclub in London.

Although Dannii had asked Fearne to set her up on a date because she said she couldn't find a boyfriend of her own, perhaps, in many ways, this could not have come at a worse time. Already she was being romantically linked to Simon Cowell, although both of them had never suggested they were anything more than just friends and colleagues. Neither had it helped that the *News of the World* had, some months earlier, revealed how millions were logging on to the Internet to watch CCTV scenes of Dannii's girl-on-girl lesbian romp with a naked lap dancer at the Puss in Boots nightspot in London.

According to the stripper, Janine Marshall, 'Dannii devoured me during that dance like a ravenous tiger.' In a *News of the World* exposé, Janine revealed how Dannii begged for her attention, groped her breasts and bum, and gawped at her naked like an excited teenager. When she arrived at the club in September 2005 with her boyfriend and another couple, Dannii immediately singled out the stripper: 'She picked me for a private dance so I led them to a quiet corner in the VIP area and they settled into the sofas. Then I began my routine.' Even though Janine concentrated on the guys in the party, she soon turned her attention to Dannii: 'She was calling out for me, so I sauntered over and squeezed my breasts as I danced seductively in front of her.'

But she had a three-foot rule – never to go closer than that with clients. With Dannii, it was different, however: 'I pushed the boundaries more than I would with other clients because she's a woman and I felt safe.' She then moved on to the star's female pal: 'I gyrated between her legs and that sent Dannii even wilder, she kicked her leg out in sheer excitement.' And when Janine started work on Dannii's boyfriend (with whom she has since split), she was transfixed: 'I kept my eyes locked on Dannii's the whole time I was dancing for him and she loved it. She was grinning like a Cheshire cat. I don't know if it turned her on seeing her man with another woman but she was totally cool with it.'

It was at that point that Janine pushed her performance up a notch: 'I teased down my skirt and was dancing in my panties and halter-neck bikini top, which I unknotted. My boobs fell out of my top and I peeled off my knickers before stepping out of them. Dannii admired me. She said, "Wow, look at that body!" I knew I looked fantastic. At one point she grabbed a curl of my hair and twiddled it around her finger. And she said, "You've got such sexy hair." Then she whispered, "You're stunning, you're turning me on so much."'

And of course, Janine knew how to turn up the heat even more. She grinned, 'Table dancing is all about the tease, so one minute I was five feet from her and the next just one millimetre separated us. I leaned towards her with my face pressed against hers, then I moved away. It was a case of, "Look at me, I'm beautiful, but you can't have me."' But Dannii didn't have to wait long to get closer. Janine explained, 'I moved nearer again, this time on my knees. Dannii adored my boobs and couldn't believe they were natural. I turned around to face a mirrored wall and as I arched my back my bottom pushed out towards Dannii,' she recalled. 'I could see her through the mirror grinning at her boyfriend, like a cat that had got the cream.'

And as if that wasn't enough, Janine then gave an X-rated on-the-floor show: 'I laid on my back and gyrated my body against the carpet. Then I kneeled on the floor and leaned back on my heels. My arms were above my head and I could see Dannii getting a good view of everything. I was totally naked. She was flicking her hair like an excitable teenager as she gawped at me.'

It was then that Janine gave Dannii, who was lying flat on the sofa by that point, a closer inspection: 'I lifted her leg up towards me and clasped my fingers around her ankle. Then I used my lips to trace a line from her ankle to the middle part of her calf. It tickled her into a frenzy because Dannii couldn't stop moving, she was too turned on to sit still.'

When the dance was over, Dannii booked Janine to sit with them for a further hour and during that time the conversation centred on one thing: stripping.

'Dannii said she loved watching me dance naked and admitted she'd had pole dancing lessons herself. She said she enjoyed pole dancing and it made her feel sexy.' Janine, who has given up lap dancing and now runs a successful agency in west London, later gave her mobile number to the star after Dannii invited her to a fashion show that night. But she never heard from her again until February 2006, after the *News of the World* revealed the video footage was on the Internet: 'She sent a message through a friend saying she hoped I was okay. It was nice of her to think of me. She was shocked and upset when the CCTV stills from her dalliance became public.' Even if it was just a bit of innocent fun, Dannii had nothing to say on the subject. Well, not publicly, anyway!

Fearne, however, was not quite so reticent on the subject of going teetotal. She had given up alcohol three months before Christmas and said she had never felt better: 'I wasn't a big drinker before so I found it quite easy to give up completely and now I feel bloody brilliant,' she told *Company* magazine when they caught up with her for a January 2008 feature, which had them wondering how she managed to look 'so darn cool'. But, she continued, she wasn't about to change her eating habits: 'I've seen pop stars on really strict diets and you can't help but wonder how they do it. I find it so sad. I'd rather be happy and have a little pot belly than be skinny and miserable.'

Not that she looked unhappy when she posed alongside a life-sized ice sculpture of herself on 8 November 2007 to celebrate being named London's Princess of Cool at the opening of the Natural History Museum ice rink that had been placed on the museum's east lawn for the third year in a row. Open from November to January, the 1,000-metre-square rink had become one of the top seasonal attractions for celebrities. In 2006, Spice Girls Victoria Beckham and Geri Halliwell were spotted practising their moves. As Fearne said at the time, 'The Natural History Museum is a breathtaking setting and makes this a special place to skate in London this winter. The rink is a great example of how the capital is literally one of the coolest cities in the world.' And yes, she did have a chance to test the ice herself.

Equally cool were the television projects that she was lining up for the New Year. One of them was a new fashion show that ITV scheduled to air in September and was already described as being like a 'Top Gear for Girls' with the Jeremy Clarkson, Richard Hammond and James May roles taken by Fearne, model Abigail Clancy and Girls Aloud's Sarah Harding. As far as ITV were concerned, the show was going to be like *Top Gear* with its challenges and reviews, and according to one source, even a 'Star in a Reasonably Priced Car' equivalent, with celebrities such as Claudia Schiffer, Stella McCartney and Lily Allen all helping out.

The idea was to pitch the female equivalent against *Top Gear* so that it would become as popular among young women as the BBC's smash hit has already proved to be with men, but according to an ITV insider, the plan was also to make it appealing to men as well. Already being hailed as the next television sensation, filming had begun in January 2008 when the news broke of its in-production status. If nothing else it would launch the television careers of Peter Crouch's girlfriend Abi and blonde bombshell Sarah Harding. 'The girls will try out dramatic outfits – some of those will be saucy, like a new G-string,' said a spokesperson.

The other show that Fearne had waiting in the wings was *Guilty Pleasures,* for ITV1, which, according to the press release that appeared on the Internet, would see: 'Some of the nation's favourite chart stars like you've never seen them before.' Craig David, Kelly Osbourne, Sophie Ellis-Bextor and Supergrass's Gaz and Danny were among the top acts lined up to perform their very own 'guilty musical pleasure' in a celebration of music that is ever so slightly shameful to love.

Fearne was recruited to host the proceedings and it was perfect for her:'Presenting *Guilty Pleasures* is going to be the best fun. What a great combination of cool bands, artists and all my fave tunes! I'm going to make sure I find the time to have a little dance as well.' It was a one-off special that would air in April at some point, she revealed, but in actual fact it ended up being shown in March. After filming, she was equally enthusiastic as when she was first told about the idea: 'It was sooooooooooooo fun! Basically we had bunch of cool folk such as KT Tunstall, Kelly Osbourne, Supergrass, performing their fave cheesy classics! The audience were well up for it and danced all night! Kelly O rocked it ... she was cackin' it but totally rocked with her version of Bonnie Tyler's "Total Eclipse of the Heart".'

The concept was the brainchild of the show's creator Sean Rowley, who had started out his *Guilty Pleasures* idea as an affront to music snobs everywhere, giving airplay to great pop tunes for simply being that: great pop tunes, whether they were on the wrong side of cool or not. He's since taken *Guilty Pleasures* to another level with his festival appearances and infamous club nights, which have been described as a 'global phenomenon'. It was why he was bringing the pleasure to the small screen: '*Guilty Pleasures* is a modern-day success story, which has, in four incredible years, entered the lexicon of everyday banter. The music played at *Guilty Pleasures* won't ever make the rock critics' Top 10s but we play it free of irony and celebrate pop music in all its glorious forms.'

And he had his own reasons why he was so keen to bring it to the screen: 'Little did I know that when I was a youngster and I'd hide certain records from my mates because I knew that they just weren't cool that this would lead to the kind of adventures I've had with *Guilty Pleasures* over the last four years. It's been a dream to see this grow into a TV show and I'm very proud, especially as it was all borne out of my secret obsession for David Cassidy and ELO!'

It would have been much the same as if one had tried to compare Elvis Presley's *Double Trouble* album with *Sgt Pepper's Lonely Hearts Club Band* by the Beatles. Although both were released during the same month in 1967, they were simply light years away from each other. Elvis singing 'Old MacDonald' was never going to be quite so cool as 'Lucy In The Sky With Diamonds' – it just wasn't feasible.

Proving a much greater hotbed of inspiration than Elvis for Fearne was when she landed her biggest coup yet: hosting *The Guinness Book of Records Live: Top 100!* for the NBC network in America. She flew to Los Angeles for five days of rehearsals before the show aired on Sunday, 27 January 2008. Featuring a countdown of the 100 Greatest Guinness World Records in history, including some of the most memorable and wacky records ever attempted, such as Longest Fingernails, Longest Freefall Parachute Jump and the Most Time Spent in Space, among others, the two-hour show culminated at Universal City with a live stunt of the longest motorcycle tunnel of fire performed live for the first time on US television by expert stunt rider Clint Ewing, who attempted to beat the current record of 178 feet by 22 feet. And he did!

It is interesting to ponder why Fearne, who is relatively unknown in the States, had been picked for the show ahead of a string of more established home-grown presenters, however. According to most industry insiders, on both sides of the Atlantic, 'It was a huge opportunity for her. Loads of British stars try to make it in Hollywood but only a few ever succeed.'

Rob Molloy, Director of Television at Guinness World Records, agreed: 'This commission with one of America's biggest networks shows the huge appeal of working with the Guinness World Records brand on TV. The versatility of our content means it can be tailored for almost any channel and audience and we hope success with this show will lead to more collaborations between us and NBC in 2008.'

Although Cat Deeley has been one of those who preceded Fearne with moderate success in such American shows as *So You Think You Can Dance* and stepping into the *Tonight Show with Jay Leno* when Leno wasn't available, it is going to be interesting to see if Fearne can follow the same path with equal or even more success in a country where it is not so easy to get that big break.

One week after the Guinness show aired, Fearne announced that she had quit *The Xtra Factor* after landing her second dream job on US television. According to 'friends', she had apparently outgrown the programme and was far more interested in concentrating on her new talent show in America: 'She had fun working on *The Xtra Factor* but she has decided to quit while she was ahead. There was no guarantee she would have been doing a second series anyway. It made sense to make a clean break and concentrate on America. There's no bad blood there but they didn't exactly get on like a house on fire.'

She hoped she would feel more at home with her colleagues while working on her new programme, *Last Comic Standing*. This time she would be co-hosting the show that sets out across America and Canada to discover their funniest comedians. It had been on air in the States since 2003 and to this day mixes elements of *American Idol* and *Survivor* as contestants share a house and choose their opponents in head-to-head competitions decided by their audience, with the winner copping an NBC talent deal.

Filming auditions in February 2008, she travelled to Los Angeles, New York City and Miami; by the time Valentine's Day arrived she was in Canada. But even though the idea of finding funny people had been fun, weird and wonderful, she admitted, 'Obviously I have met a lot of people who are not funny, which in itself *can* be funny!' When she was in Canada, it was minus six degrees when she had a day off, but being a lone traveller, she was bored and had no intention of stepping out into the snow. If anything, she was more excited about returning home and was looking forward to doing 'all the backstage stuff again' at the *Brits*: 'It's gonna be a massive night, what with the Osbournes hosting! I love them and cannot wait! I adore Sharon but am yet to meet Ozzie – should be a wicked night!' And she was right: it was.

Among the acts performing at the mega bash were Kylie, Mark Ronson, Mika, Rihanna, Kaiser Chiefs, Leona Lewis, Amy Winehouse and the winner of the Outstanding Contribution to Music Award, Sir Paul McCartney.

Although Kylie was again being dubbed the 'Queen of the Brits' and walked away with 'Best International Female Solo Artist', it was not quite the same as 2002 when she landed two of the gongs for which she had been nominated and gave a brilliant remixed performance of 'Can't Get You Out of My Head', then the triumph of the evening, when she came sliding out of an escalating giant CD with the then-famous KYLIE logo spelt out in fluorescent pink behind her. Whether presenting, receiving her 2008 prize from *Doctor Who* ally David Tennant or performing her then latest single 'Wow', six years earlier when she was dressed in a white Dolce & Gabbana basque, silver boots just up over her knees and matching silver knickers, writhing her way through her chart-topper cleverly blended with New Order's dance classic 'Blue Monday', it could not have been bettered. At the same time, Fearne was swanning around the *Brits*' after-show parties in an equally daring ensemble: bright, two-piece red hot pants – the talk of the night.

One has to wonder if, at this time, Fearne might be considering where her own future was to take her. It is perhaps questionable whether, if she does follow in the footsteps of Cat Deeley and other British presenters that have made it big in the States, she would decide to move out there for good. Although that has yet to be seen, it does seem unlikely that she will take that step.

Immediately after *The Brits*, she flew back out to the States to continue working on *Last Comic Standing*. 'This time we went to Texas (no veggie food to be seen), Arizona (hot, hot, hot), San Fran (groovy, groovy), and Nashville (yeah, I went line dancing),' she told her MySpace friends. 'It was a mad rush to each city and once again I met some very interesting characters!! Man dressed as a monkey, banana man, and an incredible hulk in Lycra!! Nashville was probably my favourite stop this time. I learnt how to hoola hoop, aged 26, had the best homemade ice-cream ever, and line danced with the country folk!'

But when she got home, she was 'zombied' she says. 'I was so shattered when I got in, I turned in to a bit of a nut and cleaned the whole house to stay awake. Why not just have a coffee I hear you cry? I did have three when I landed so I guess that explains the go gadget cleaning!!'

And in another blog she wrote on Easter Saturday, she told a story explaining why it is never a good idea to laugh at your mates; a lesson that she admits to learning the hard way. 'About 3 months ago I went to Bikrham yoga with my mate Jake. Jake is about six foot four, and all I have to do is look at him to laugh. He is always goofing around and causing a riot in most situations! By the way, Bikrham yoga is like doing an exercise class in a sauna ... No, make that hell. That's how hot it is! So after ten minutes, Jake is sitting on the mat mouthing to me, "I'm gonna be sick!" I laughed inside and ignored him so I could stay in the yoga zone. I thought poor Jakey was fooling around for a laugh. He looked pretty green at the end of the class and I ribbed him about this for so long!!'

Cut to what she calls the most embarrassing moment of her life, when she attempted the class again, one week before Easter, 'This time taking my good friend Lolly! I told her how horrid yet satisfying it was going to be and, of course, told her all about Jake retching on his yoga mat! So we start doing some stretches and I start feeling very odd. I try to ignore this strong car sickness sensation though. The next thing I know I'm laying flat on my side, dizzy as can be. Yep, I fainted at Bikrham yoga!!! In front of about thirty people who were currently in very complex yogic poses! Cringee!! I kept mouthing to the instructor "I'm gonna be sick" ... she mouths back "stay there" ... all I wanted to do was run out of the class and never be seen again. But she would not let me leave. After about ten minutes I felt a little better and managed to do the rest of the class but a little half heartedly to be honest!! Instant bloody karma!! I, of course, called Jake straight after and told him the complete account of what happened and he was thrilled! So, no, never laugh at your mates,' she repeated.

Yoga sagas aside, Fearne generally prefers to keep her life as uncomplicated as possible. And with the Victorian house that she has recently bought in her favourite 'leafy part' of south-west London, the Mini Cooper she loves to tear around in (she says she is always late), the friends she spends so much time with when she isn't on-camera, not to mention the unique gigs and festivals in and around London that she attends and enjoys so much, would she ever, really, consider packing her bags and quitting the city that she describes as the coolest place on earth? Of course, if she did decide to settle in Los Angeles, Beverly Hills or Hollywood, would she really be happy to leave behind her parents, brother Jamie and her two cats, even if she did travel back and forth as regular as clockwork? It just wouldn't be the same.

It's unlikely that she would want to leave any of that behind, even though she has an American boyfriend. Already Jesse is spending most of his time in Britain, so what would be the point, apart from gaining even more of the fame and fortune that she perhaps wouldn't embrace? Undoubtedly, she would be more hounded in America than in Britain and she might also have to consider how she would feel about spending the rest of her youth basking in the flashbulbs of Hollywood's ravenous paparazzi. As she has already been described as guarded, secretive and intensely private, she would have to kiss goodbye to her private life and, no matter how driven or ambitious she appears to be, is she really the kind of celebrity to put her career before everything else that she loves and adores? Even though she now makes part of her living in Hollywood, it doesn't mean she has to live her life there as well!

Chronology: 1981–2008

3 September 1981

Fearne Marie Cotton is born in north London.

1986

She starts ballet lessons.

1996

She starts weekend drama school.

1998

She attends an audition and lands a presenting job with GMTV hosting *The Disney Club*.

March 1998

Diggit starts its runs on GMTV with Fearne co-presenting with Paul 'Des' Ballard.

July 1998

She is pictured in the *Radio Times* in her school uniform. The article is about how she and co-presenter Paul 'Des' Ballard juggle their presenting work with school.

October 1998

With co-presenter Jim Jenkins, she presents the first episode of *Draw Your Own Toons,* a children's daytime series that looks at how cartoons are made.

February 1999

She hosts first episode of the *Pump It Up* series, a children's game show in which teams of kids face a series of physical challenges set in a huge inflatable arena.

July 2000

She presents the first episode of *Mouse,* an audience participation series for children all about using the Internet.

January 2001

ITV airs the first episode of *Finger Tips*, a children's daytime art and craft series that Fearne co-presents with Stephen Mulhern.

March 2001

She starts the run of presenting *Petswap*, a children's daytime game show in which contestants swap places with pets.

September 2001

First show with CBBC. She joins Kate Heavenor to co-present the children's science series, *Eureka*.

September 2002

Joins Reggie Yates, an upcoming presenter, to host *Smile*, a children's interactive series featuring guests, competitions and games. It is aired on BBC2.

February 2003

Guests on *Never Mind The Buzzcocks* on BBC2 with Sarah Whatmore, Dennis Locorriere and Christian Datsun.

March 2003

Becomes the second celebrity to be voted off *Comic Relief Does Fame Academy* on BBC1 after she gives a poor rendition of the Travis song, 'Driftwood'.

September 2003

Presents *Top of the Pops Saturday* with Simon Grant as part of *The Saturday Show* on BBC1, which she and Simon take over from Dani Behr and Jo Mace.

October 2003

The *Sun* reports that Fearne is secretly dating *Fame Academy* contestant Peter Brame. It is the start of an intense and often unstable relationship.

November 2003

Appears in the video for the official *Children In Need* single, 'I'm Your Man' by Shane Ritchie (she is seen as the barmaid with whom Shane flirts). She co-hosts the telethon with Terry Wogan and Natasha Kaplinsky.

December 2003

Appears as Sleeping Beauty in the BBC production of *Sleeping Beauty Uncovered*.

June 2004

The relationship with Brame ends.

July 2004

Takes part in *Sports Relief* and joins Nigel Harman, Andrew Marr, Sarah Manners and Nick Knowles to represent the BBC team for a special star-studded episode of *Superstars: Battle of the Channels*.

August 2004

Meets Ian Watkins of Lostprophets at the *Kerrang!* Awards and starts a relationship. She also attends the

V2004 Festival in Weston Park, Staffordshire and Chelmsford, Essex, with Christopher Parker.

January 2005
Narrates the second series of *Serious*, observational documentaries for CBBC.

March 2005
Visits Kenya with Christopher Parker to see how Comic Relief are working to help tackle poverty, abuse and social injustice. Presents *Make Me A Supermodel* on ITV1 and kicks off the first hour of *Red Nose Day* with Jonathan Ross on BBC1.

April 2005
Joins cowboy tribute band the Sunset Pioneers and plays washboard for an episode she films of *Only In America*.

July 2005
She is the backstage interviewer at the Live 8 concert in Hyde Park, transmitted live on BBC1. During her interview with Robbie Williams, he asks her, live on camera, if she will go and live with him and his dogs in Los Angeles. Peter Brame sells intimate revelations of his relationship with Fearne to the *News of the World*.

September 2005

She continues to present *Top of the Pops* as it moves from the regular BBC1 Friday slot to Sundays on BBC2. From episode twelve onwards a new feature is introduced where digital viewers can press their red button to access a different choice of music. She makes a guest appearance as herself on children's television drama *Byker Grove*.

October 2005

CBBC screens Fearne and Reggie's road trip series, *Only In America*.

November 2005

She signs up for MySpace and decides to log on regularly to share her blogs, blurbs, pictures, interests, music and other MySpace stuff with about 60,000 MySpace friends. She hosts the BBC's annual telethon for *Children In Need*, with Terry Wogan and Natasha Kaplinsky.

January 2006

She features on the inside pages of *Arena*, the popular British lads' magazine. Her name is linked in the British press with Green Day drummer Tre Cool after they are seen shopping together in London's Bond Street.

February 2006

Begins dating the Kooks' lead singer Luke Pritchard.

May 2006

Announces the United Kingdom vote for the 2006 Eurovision Song Contest, held in Athens, Greece. Splits with boyfriend Luke Pritchard.

June 2006

While in Los Angeles is introduced to Jesse Jenkins, a part-time model and wannabe chef. She returns in late summer to start a relationship.

July 2006

Replaces Kelly Brook for the second series of *Celebrity Love Island*, a reality series featuring a group of single celebrities looking for romance on a tropical island, which is renamed *Love Island* and is co-presented with Patrick Kielty on ITV1. She films the introduction for the last episode of *Top of the Pops*.

August 2006

Returns to Los Angeles to pick up her relationship with Jesse Jenkins.

September 2006

Starts the BBC Radio 1 weekend breakfast broadcast with Reggie Yates. They replace Spoony, who was leaving the station after six years service.

October 2006

She appears with her family in a special star edition of game show *Family Fortunes*.

November 2006

She helps Terry Wogan and Natasha Kaplinsky host the BBC's annual *Children In Need* telethon on BBC1.

December 2006

Features on the cover of *CosmoGirl* magazine. Also presents the Christmas Day special edition of *Top of the Pops*.

January 2007

Celebrates the New Year with a 1950s fancy dress party for friends at her home in south-west London. She describes it as 'debauched and chaotic'.

February 2007

She presents *The Oscars Red Carpet Live* from outside the Kodak Theater in Hollywood for Sky One. She is the backstage presenter at the *Brit Awards*, interviewing performers when it goes out live on ITV1. Features on the covers of *Company* and *Weekend* magazines.

March 2007

She co-hosts *Making Your Mind Up* to decide which act the UK will send to the *Eurovision Song Contest* in Helsinki, Finland. She saves the blushes of her co-presenter when Terry Wogan accidentally announces the wrong artist as the winner.

May 2007

The *Sun* newspaper announces that Fearne is taking over from Ben Shephard as the host for *The X Factor* spin-off programme, *The Xtra Factor* on ITV2. She is at the Eurovision Song Contest in Helsinki, Finland, as the face for the UK vote. It falls to her to announce the highest award of 12 points to Turkey. She attends Lily Allen's launch of her clothing collection, and the after-party at the Groucho Club in London.

June 2007

The BBC show Fearne's interview with Princes William and Harry that was filmed at Clarence House. She appears on *Friday Night with Jonathan Ross*.

July 2007

She interviews performers and guests backstage at the Concert for Diana at the new Wembley Stadium. She launches her own range of organic cotton clothes that are aimed at music festival-goers.

August 2007

Features on the cover of *Live*, the *Mail on Sunday* magazine, surrounded by flying vinyl. She also appears on the inside pages of *GQ* magazine in a series of sexy poses. Plays bridesmaid to best friend Holly Willoughby at her wedding to Dan Baldwin, television producer. Becomes the new presenter of *The Xtra Factor* on ITV2.

September 2007

Presents the first episode of *Holly and Fearne Go Dating* on ITV1 with Holly Willoughby. She also becomes patron of the PostPals charity, an organisation that brightens the lives of seriously ill children. She and Holly *Beat the Boys* by 20 seconds on *Ant and Dec's Saturday Night Takeaway* by completing an assault course in a beach buggy.

October 2007

Becomes the first-ever permanent female presenter of the *Radio 1 Chart Show*, which she co-presents with Reggie Yates. They take over from JK & Joel. The show now includes a rundown of the Top 40 singles and downloads, and live/studio chat with artists and bands. She starts the weekend request show with Reggie. She and Holly Willoughby accept the National Television Award for 'Most Popular Entertainment Presenter' on behalf of Ant and Dec at London's Royal Albert Hall.

November 2007

Hosts the *Cosmopolitan* magazine's 'Ultimate Woman of the Year' Awards at the Cirque in London. Unveils a life-sized ice sculpture of herself to celebrate being named London's princess of cool at the opening of the Natural History Museum ice rink.

December 2007

Travels to India to witness the work being done in Chennai by World Vision and the Street Children Project. She is named as the official ambassador for the 24-hour famine campaign 2008. Hosts a Christmas special for ITV1 of the best and worst auditions from *The X Factor* series.

January 2008

Arrives in Los Angeles to begin rehearsals for the live broadcast of *The Guinness World Records Top 100* for the American NBC network. The show goes out five days later. Films a one-off music special for ITV1 called *Guilty Pleasures*, which stars, among others, Kelly Osbourne, Sophie Ellis-Bextor and KT Tunstall performing songs that are not considered cool.

February 2008

Features on the cover of *Company*, the fashion, beauty and celebrity magazine. Voted the third ultimate fantasy woman for foot fetishists, behind Kylie and Angelina Jolie. She quits *The Xtra Factor* and wins a deal to front *Last Comic Standing* in the US and films auditions for the show in Los Angeles, New York City, Miami and Canada. She returns to London to be the backstage presenter for the *Brit Awards* at Earl's Court.

Television and Radio

This listing of Fearne's television and radio shows relates only to the programmes she has presented/hosted/co-hosted and does not include miscellaneous appearances. The data was compiled from information logged at the British Film Institute in London and from the Internet Movie Database (imdb.com).

1998: *The Disney Club* (GMTV)
     Draw Your Own Toons (GMTV)
     Diggit/Diggin' It (GMTV)

1999: *Pump It Up* (ITV)
     Draw Your Own Toons (GMTV)

2000: *Mouse* (ITV)
     Draw Your Own Toons (GMTV)
     Pump It Up (ITV)

2001: *Draw Your Own Toons* (GMTV)
Petswap (ITV)
Record Breakers (BBC1)
Mouse (ITV)

2002: *Finger Tips* (ITV1)
Smile (CBBC)
The Saturday Show (BBC1)
Eureka (BBC1)

2003: *Finger Tips* (ITV1)
Smile (CBBC)
The Saturday Show (BBC1)
Top of the Pops Saturday (BBC1)
Comic Relief Does Fame Academy (BBC1)
Children In Need (BBC1)

2004: *Finger Tips* (ITV1)
Top of the Pops Reloaded (BBC1)
Top of the Pops (BBC1)

2005: *Serious* (CBBC)
Only In America (CBBC)
Live 8 (BBC1/BBC2)
Comic Relief: Red Nose Night Live (BBC1)
Top of the Pops Reloaded (BBC1)
Top of the Pops (BBC2)
Children In Need (BBC1)
The Friday Morning Show (BBC Radio 1)

2006: *Top of the Pops* (BBC2)
Make Me A Supermodel (FIVE)
Love Island (ITV1)
Eurovision Song Contest (BBC1)
Children In Need (BBC1)
The Weekend Breakfast Show (BBC Radio 1)

2007: *The Brits Are Coming* (ITV1)
The Brits (ITV1)
Comic Relief: The Big One (BBC1)
Making Your Mind Up (BBC1)
Eurovision Song Contest (BBC1)
The Oscars Red Carpet Live (SKY)
The British Soap Awards (ITV1)
Concert for Diana: The Princes' Interview (BBC1)
Concert for Diana (BBC1)
Holly and Fearne Go Dating (ITV1)
The Xtra Factor (ITV2)
Children In Need (BBC1)
Best Ever Worst Auditions (ITV1)
The Weekend Breakfast Show (BBC Radio 1)
Radio 1 Chart Show (BBC Radio 1)

2008: *The Guinness Book of Records Live!* (NBC)
The Brits (ITV1)
Guilty Pleasures (ITV1)
Last Comic Standing (NBC)
Top Gear For Girls (ITV1)
Reggie and Fearne's Request Show (BBC Radio 1)
Radio 1 Chart Show (BBC Radio 1)

The following books by Nigel Goodall can now be purchased from your local bookshop or direct from his publisher:

Ray Winstone – The Biography
ISBN 978 1 84454 383 0   HB   £17.99

The Secret World of Johnny Depp
ISBN 978 1 84454 387 8   PB   £7.99

Being Davina
ISBN 978 1 84454 385 4   PB   £7.99

Christian Slater – The Biography
ISBN 978 1 84454 137 9   HB   £17.99

Free P+P and UK Delivery
(Abroad £3.00 per book)

TO ORDER SIMPLY CALL THIS NUMBER
+ 44 (0) 207 381 0666

Or visit our website www.blake.co.uk

Prices and availability subject to change without notice

DAVID TENNANT
A LIFE IN TIME AND SPACE

Nigel Goodall

David Tennant is the most powerful actor on British television. And, with two National Television awards to his credit and numerous other theatrical accolades, David has proven he's here to stay.

The son of a Presbyterian minister, David was raised in the small suburban settlement of Ralston in Scotland. He appeared on screen before he was even out of school. Then, after graduating from drama school, he landed his first professional acting role in the theatrical production of *The Resistible Rise of Arturo Uiith*. This was just the beginning of what has since become a distinguished acting career.

David has appeared in several high-profile dramas for the BBC. But, undeniably, it is his energetic and eccentric portrayal of the Time Lord in cult sci-fi drama *Doctor Who* for which he is most famous. Fulfilling his childhood dream, David has been voted 'Best Doctor' by readers of *Doctor Who Magazine* and the 'coolest character' on UK television in a 2007 *Radio Times* survey.

In this, the first ever biography of the charismatic Scottish actor, Nigel Goodall traces the events and circumstances that have shaped David's life and career so far and transformed him into a hugely influential artist, and the coolest man on television.

ISBN 978 1 84454 636 7

John Blake Publishing Ltd

COMING SOON